Urban Bioeconomy: Advancing Circular Economy, Renewable Energy, Waste Management, Sustainable Agriculture, Green Infrastructure, and Biotechnology in Cities

Copyright

Urban Bioeconomy: Advancing Circular Economy, Renewable Energy, Waste Management, Sustainable Agriculture, Green Infrastructure, and Biotechnology in Cities

ISBN (eBook): 978-1-991368-29-4

ISBN (Paperback): 978-1-991368-30-0

Published by Global Climate Solutions

First Edition, 2025

Cover design and interior layout by Global Climate Solutions

Table of Contents

Introduction

The concept of the urban bioeconomy offers an innovative pathway for cities to transition toward sustainable and regenerative systems that mirror the cycles of nature. With urban populations expanding at unprecedented rates, the demand for resources such as food, water, and energy continues to grow, often outpacing the capacity of traditional systems to supply them sustainably. The urban bioeconomy emerges as a response to these pressures, creating opportunities to rethink how cities produce, consume, and recycle resources in ways that prioritize biological processes, reduce waste, and replace fossil-based inputs with renewable alternatives.

At its core, the urban bioeconomy is built on principles of circularity, resilience, and innovation. Unlike linear models of extraction, production, consumption, and disposal, the bioeconomy emphasizes closed-loop systems where organic materials are reused and nutrients are cycled back into productive systems. Cities, with their concentration of people, industries, and infrastructure, are uniquely positioned to apply these principles at scale. By integrating bioeconomic thinking into urban planning, industries, and services, municipalities can turn challenges such as waste generation, pollution, and resource scarcity into opportunities for sustainable growth and regeneration.

Urban areas are more than centers of economic activity; they are also hubs of creativity and experimentation. The dense networks of institutions, businesses, and communities that exist in cities provide fertile ground for bioeconomic innovation. For example, the development of bio-based construction materials, waste-to-energy systems, or circular food systems can be accelerated in cities where demand and investment potential are highest. The urban bioeconomy also fosters collaboration across multiple sectors—bringing together policymakers, researchers, entrepreneurs, and citizens to co-create solutions that are both economically viable and environmentally restorative.

Another key element of the urban bioeconomy is the role of technology and biotechnology. Advances in biotechnology, synthetic biology, and digital innovation are unlocking new possibilities for how biological resources can be harnessed and managed. From precision agriculture in urban farming to bio-based plastics and advanced water treatment systems, the urban bioeconomy integrates high-tech solutions with natural processes. This convergence enables cities to become not just consumers of resources but producers of renewable and regenerative value.

The socio-economic dimension of the urban bioeconomy is equally significant. Transitioning to a bio-based urban economy creates new types of jobs, fosters green entrepreneurship, and offers opportunities for social inclusion. By investing in education and workforce development, cities can prepare citizens for roles in emerging industries tied to bio-based manufacturing, renewable energy, and circular food systems. This shift contributes not only to environmental sustainability but also to economic resilience and social equity, ensuring that the benefits of the transition are widely shared.

Governance plays a critical role in guiding the urban bioeconomy. Effective policies, incentives, and regulatory frameworks are needed to encourage innovation, attract investment, and align local initiatives with national and international sustainability goals. Equally important is the engagement of citizens, who must be empowered to participate in and support new forms of consumption, recycling, and community-based initiatives. Without public buy-in and inclusive governance, the transition to an urban bioeconomy cannot succeed.

Ultimately, the urban bioeconomy represents a vision for cities that thrive within planetary boundaries. It is not simply about adopting new technologies or substituting fossil-based inputs with renewable ones; it is about fundamentally rethinking the role of cities in global sustainability. By aligning economic activity with the regenerative capacities of ecosystems, the urban bioeconomy provides a roadmap for building cities that are adaptive, resilient, and prosperous in the face of 21st-century challenges.

Chapter 1: Foundations of the Urban Bioeconomy

The urban bioeconomy represents a transformative vision for cities, reorienting growth around biological resources, circularity, and regenerative practices. As urban areas expand, they become centers of resource consumption, waste generation, and innovation, making them critical spaces for bioeconomic transitions. Understanding the foundations of the urban bioeconomy involves clarifying its concepts, historical evolution, and guiding principles. This chapter establishes the groundwork by defining the bioeconomy, tracing its shift from traditional practices to urban applications, and identifying key ideas such as biological circularity and systems thinking. Together, these foundations provide the framework for building sustainable and resilient cities.

Defining the Bioeconomy

The bioeconomy can be broadly defined as an economic model that relies on the sustainable use of biological resources, processes, and principles to produce goods and services. It moves beyond fossil-based and linear systems by embedding renewable resources, circularity, and ecological thinking into the core of economic activity. At its foundation, the bioeconomy draws on renewable biological inputs such as crops, forests, marine resources, and organic waste, as well as biotechnology and ecosystem services, to create value while maintaining the integrity of natural systems.

Historically, economies have been dependent on extracting finite resources to fuel growth, resulting in environmental degradation and climate change. The bioeconomy offers an alternative path by aligning production and consumption with the regenerative capacities of nature. Rather than treating biological materials as disposable, the bioeconomy emphasizes their reuse, recycling, and transformation into higher-value products. This includes converting organic waste into energy, using biomass for bio-based plastics, and developing biotechnologies that improve efficiency and reduce environmental impact.

Central to the bioeconomy is circularity. In contrast to linear "take-make-dispose" models, circular systems ensure that biological resources flow continuously through economic processes. Organic matter that once would have been discarded is reintegrated as feedstock, fertilizer, or energy. This reduces dependence on non-renewable inputs, cuts greenhouse gas emissions, and strengthens resilience against resource scarcity. The bioeconomy thus enables societies to meet human needs without overshooting ecological limits.

The scope of the bioeconomy is vast, encompassing sectors such as agriculture, forestry, fisheries, food production, energy, chemicals, pharmaceuticals, and construction. Biotechnology plays a key role, enabling innovations such as genetically optimized crops, bio-based materials, and advanced medical therapies. These innovations expand the range of bio-based products available, reduce reliance on petrochemicals, and open new avenues for sustainable growth. Importantly, the bioeconomy is not limited to high-technology applications; it also includes traditional practices like composting, sustainable forestry, and organic farming, which embody bioeconomic principles.

Social and economic dimensions are integral to defining the bioeconomy. It has the potential to generate green jobs, create new industries, and strengthen rural and urban economies. By supporting small-scale producers, entrepreneurs, and community initiatives, the bioeconomy fosters inclusivity and local empowerment. At the same time, it offers opportunities for large-scale industries to shift toward more sustainable models. Education, workforce training, and citizen participation are critical to ensuring that the transition to a bioeconomy benefits society broadly.

Governance provides the framework for the bioeconomy to thrive. Policies, regulations, and incentives shape markets, encourage investment, and align innovation with sustainability goals. International cooperation supports the development of standards, research partnerships, and trade in bio-based goods. At the local level, municipalities can integrate bioeconomy principles into planning, infrastructure, and waste management, embedding biological thinking into urban systems.

In essence, the bioeconomy redefines how societies interact with natural resources. It is not merely a substitution of renewable for non-renewable inputs but a systemic transformation of economic activity to mirror the regenerative logic of ecosystems. By placing biology and circularity at the center of development, the bioeconomy lays the foundation for economies that are both prosperous and sustainable.

The Evolution from Traditional to Urban Bioeconomy

The roots of the bioeconomy can be traced back to traditional societies that relied heavily on biological resources for survival and development. Early economies were predominantly bio-based, dependent on agriculture, forestry, fisheries, and the use of natural materials for food, shelter, and energy. These systems operated within ecological limits, with cycles of production and consumption closely tied to seasonal rhythms and the regenerative capacities of ecosystems. In many cases, practices such as composting, crop rotation, and local material use reflected an implicit understanding of biological circularity, even if they were not framed in modern sustainability terms.

The industrial revolution marked a turning point, shifting economies away from renewable biological inputs toward fossil fuels and synthetic materials. This transition allowed for rapid industrialization, urbanization, and economic growth, but it also disconnected societies from ecological cycles. Fossil-based systems encouraged a linear "take-make-dispose" model, with little regard for resource regeneration or waste management. Cities, in particular, became centers of consumption and pollution, driving demand for materials and energy that exceeded local ecological capacities. While traditional bio-based practices persisted in rural areas, they were marginalized by the dominance of fossil-fuel economies.

In recent decades, mounting environmental pressures have prompted a renewed focus on biological resources as part of the solution to sustainability challenges. Climate change, biodiversity loss, pollution, and resource depletion have exposed the vulnerabilities of fossil-based systems. At the same time, advances in biotechnology, digitalization, and circular economy thinking have opened new opportunities to reimagine how biological resources can be sustainably integrated into modern economies. This shift represents not a simple return to traditional bio-based practices but the emergence of a new bioeconomy, shaped by innovation, science, and global sustainability goals.

The urban bioeconomy represents the next stage in this evolution, uniquely tailored to the realities of 21st-century cities. Unlike traditional bioeconomy models, which were often rural and resource-extractive, the urban bioeconomy emphasizes circularity within densely populated environments. Cities are no longer just centers of consumption; they are re-envisioned as hubs of production, innovation, and regeneration. Organic waste streams, previously considered burdens, are transformed into valuable inputs for energy, fertilizers, and bio-based products. Urban agriculture, vertical farming, and aquaponics integrate food production into city landscapes, reducing dependence on distant supply chains.

Another hallmark of the urban bioeconomy is its integration with advanced technology. Biotechnology enables the creation of bio-based materials and fuels, while digital tools optimize resource flows and track circular processes. Smart waste management systems, bio-refineries located near urban centers, and bio-based construction materials exemplify how the bioeconomy has adapted to urban contexts. These innovations allow cities to move beyond traditional resource dependency, embedding biological and circular logic into infrastructure, industry, and everyday life.

Governance has also evolved to support the transition. While traditional bio-based economies operated largely without formal policy frameworks, the urban bioeconomy is shaped by deliberate strategies, regulations, and investments aimed at fostering sustainability. National policies, municipal planning, and international frameworks now align to support bioeconomic innovation in urban areas. This structured approach ensures that the urban bioeconomy not only addresses environmental challenges but also contributes to economic development and social inclusion.

In summary, the evolution from traditional to urban bioeconomy reflects a trajectory from subsistence-based systems, through fossil-fueled industrialization, to technologically advanced, circular models embedded in cities. The urban bioeconomy builds on the principles of traditional bio-based practices but integrates them with modern science, innovation, and governance, making it a cornerstone of sustainable urban futures.

Key Principles of Biological Circularity

Biological circularity refers to the design and management of economic systems in ways that align with the regenerative cycles of nature. It emphasizes the continuous cycling of biological resources, ensuring that organic materials are not wasted but returned to productive use in ecosystems or transformed into valuable new inputs. At its core, biological circularity is about recognizing that biological resources are renewable when managed within ecological limits and that natural systems provide models for designing resilient, efficient, and sustainable economies.

The first principle of biological circularity is resource regeneration. Natural ecosystems operate by renewing their components over time—forests regrow, soils replenish nutrients, and water cycles refresh supplies. In the bioeconomy, this principle translates into practices that ensure resources such as biomass, water, and nutrients are managed in ways that allow for continuous regeneration. It requires balancing consumption with replenishment so that human activities do not exceed the regenerative capacity of ecosystems.

The second principle is cascading use of biological materials. In biological circularity, resources are not used once and discarded but are applied in multiple stages of value creation. For example, biomass can be first used for food production, then repurposed into bio-based materials, and finally converted into energy or compost at the end of its life cycle. This cascading approach maximizes the utility of biological resources while minimizing waste, aligning economic processes with natural cycles of transformation.

A third principle is closing nutrient and energy loops. Biological systems thrive because nutrients and energy flow continuously through cycles, supporting growth and renewal. Applying this principle to urban and industrial systems involves capturing organic waste, wastewater, and byproducts, and reintegrating them into productive uses. Technologies such as anaerobic digestion, composting, and advanced water treatment exemplify how nutrients and energy can be recovered and recirculated, reducing dependence on external inputs while minimizing pollution.

The fourth principle is designing for biodegradability and renewal. Products and processes within the bioeconomy must be designed with their end-of-life in mind, ensuring that they can be safely reintegrated into natural systems. This involves favoring materials that are biodegradable, recyclable, or reusable without generating harmful residues. By adopting design principles inspired by nature, economies can reduce environmental burdens and create regenerative product life cycles.

The fifth principle is symbiosis between human and natural systems. Biological circularity acknowledges that human economies are embedded within larger ecological systems. Rather than exploiting nature as an external resource, this principle emphasizes integrating human activity into ecological processes in mutually supportive ways. Examples include urban agriculture that enhances biodiversity, green infrastructure that manages water sustainably, and biorefineries that function as part of urban ecosystems.

Finally, the principle of resilience through diversity underscores that circular biological systems thrive when they incorporate a variety of resources, processes, and actors. Just as ecosystems are resilient when diverse, bioeconomic systems are more adaptable when they include multiple sources of biomass, varied applications, and diverse stakeholders. This diversity reduces vulnerabilities and strengthens the capacity to withstand shocks, whether environmental, economic, or social.

Together, these principles provide a framework for aligning economic activity with the regenerative logic of natural systems. They transform biological resources from finite commodities into elements of continuous cycles, offering a pathway to sustainable and resilient urban and industrial economies.

Systems Thinking in Urban Sustainability

Systems thinking is an approach that views cities not as isolated sectors or independent components but as interconnected systems where flows of energy, water, materials, people, and information continuously interact. In the context of urban sustainability, this perspective is vital because the challenges cities face—climate change, resource scarcity, pollution, and social inequality—are deeply interconnected. Addressing them effectively requires recognizing how actions in one area influence outcomes in another and designing solutions that account for the whole system rather than isolated parts.

At the heart of systems thinking is the recognition that urban environments are complex adaptive systems. Cities consist of interdependent subsystems such as transportation, housing, energy, food, and water, each of which relies on the others to function. For example, water use affects energy consumption through pumping and treatment, while food systems depend on water and energy

14

inputs. By applying systems thinking, policymakers, planners, and communities can identify feedback loops, synergies, and trade-offs that traditional linear planning approaches often overlook. This creates opportunities for more integrated and resilient solutions.

One of the key insights from systems thinking is the role of feedback loops in shaping urban sustainability. Positive feedback loops can amplify both beneficial and harmful trends, such as the way energy efficiency improvements reduce demand and lower emissions, or conversely, how urban sprawl increases car dependency and greenhouse gas emissions. Negative feedback loops, such as regulations that limit pollution or water use, help stabilize urban systems and prevent them from exceeding ecological limits. Understanding and designing for these feedback loops ensures that interventions lead to lasting improvements rather than unintended consequences.

Another principle of systems thinking in urban sustainability is the identification of leverage points—strategic areas within a system where targeted interventions can create disproportionately large benefits. For example, investing in public transit not only reduces traffic congestion but also lowers emissions, improves air quality, and enhances social inclusion. Similarly, promoting green infrastructure improves stormwater management while also providing biodiversity benefits and recreational spaces. By focusing on leverage points, cities can maximize the impact of limited resources and drive systemic change.

Collaboration across sectors is essential when applying systems thinking. Urban sustainability cannot be advanced by focusing on energy, water, waste, or housing in isolation. Cross-sectoral strategies that align infrastructure planning, governance, and community participation are more effective. For instance, integrating food, water, and energy planning highlights synergies that reduce resource use and enhance resilience. This holistic perspective ensures that policies do not shift problems from one sector to another but instead generate co-benefits across the system.

Ultimately, systems thinking fosters resilience in urban sustainability. By acknowledging complexity and interdependence, cities can anticipate shocks, adapt to changing conditions, and recover more effectively. Whether responding to climate extremes, economic disruptions, or demographic shifts, systems-oriented strategies enable cities to design flexible solutions that endure over time. In this way, systems thinking provides not only a conceptual framework but also a practical toolkit for creating urban environments that thrive within ecological and social boundaries.

Interconnections Between Urbanization and Bioeconomic Opportunities

Urbanization is one of the defining trends of the 21st century, with more than half of the global population now living in cities and the proportion continuing to rise. This concentration of people, infrastructure, and economic activity creates significant demands for resources while simultaneously generating large volumes of waste. At the same time, urbanization provides unique opportunities to advance the bioeconomy, as cities become critical sites where biological resources, circular processes, and innovation can intersect to drive sustainable development. The close relationship between urban growth and bioeconomic opportunities lies in the ability of cities to act as both problem centers and solution hubs.

One of the most direct interconnections is the challenge of managing urban resource flows. Cities account for a significant share of global energy use, water demand, and material consumption. These flows, however, also create large waste streams that can be transformed into inputs for the bioeconomy. Organic waste from households, food systems, and industries can be converted into bioenergy, fertilizers, or biochemicals, closing nutrient and material loops that would otherwise contribute to pollution. Wastewater treatment plants can be redesigned as resource recovery hubs, extracting energy, clean water, and valuable nutrients. By rethinking resource flows through a bioeconomic lens, urbanization creates an opportunity to turn linear waste streams into circular value chains.

Urbanization also shapes consumption patterns, which in turn influence bioeconomic opportunities. Cities drive demand for food, housing, mobility, and consumer goods, creating a platform for scaling bio-based products and services. Urban populations are increasingly aware of sustainability issues, opening markets for bio-based packaging, renewable construction materials, and plant-based diets. The clustering of consumers within metropolitan regions allows for rapid adoption of new technologies and products, enabling businesses to introduce bioeconomic innovations more efficiently than in dispersed rural areas. As cultural and lifestyle trends spread outward from urban centers, the demand for bio-based alternatives can ripple across entire national economies.

Another important connection lies in the role of cities as centers of knowledge, innovation, and governance. Universities, research institutions, and technology firms concentrated in urban areas drive advances in biotechnology, materials science, and digital tools that underpin the bioeconomy. Municipal governments, often more agile than national authorities, are well positioned to pilot bioeconomic policies such as waste separation systems, circular procurement, and incentives for bio-based businesses. These urban experiments provide models that can later be replicated at broader scales. The density of stakeholders in cities also supports collaboration across public, private, and civil society sectors, accelerating the development of integrated bioeconomic ecosystems.

Urbanization further creates opportunities for reimagining infrastructure through the lens of the bioeconomy. Expanding cities require new housing, transportation systems, and utilities, which can incorporate bio-based materials and circular design principles from the outset. Vertical farming and rooftop agriculture integrate food production into urban landscapes, while green infrastructure supports biodiversity and climate resilience. As cities adapt to climate challenges, bioeconomic solutions offer pathways to reduce emissions, enhance resource efficiency, and improve quality of life for residents.

The interplay between urbanization and bioeconomic opportunities demonstrates that cities are not only consumers of resources but also engines of innovation and transformation. By leveraging dense populations, concentrated waste streams, and dynamic markets, urbanization provides the scale and urgency needed to advance the bioeconomy. In turn, the bioeconomy offers cities tools to manage growth sustainably, turning challenges into opportunities for circularity, regeneration, and resilience.

Chapter 2: Governance and Policy Frameworks

Governance and policy frameworks form the backbone of the urban bioeconomy, shaping how cities adopt, regulate, and scale bio-based systems. Effective governance provides direction, accountability, and institutional capacity, while policy frameworks supply the incentives and regulations that guide behavior and investment. In the context of rapid urbanization, cities face challenges that require coordinated action across multiple levels of government and sectors. This chapter explores how governance structures, legal frameworks, and policy instruments can foster innovation, support stakeholder collaboration, and create enabling environments where the bioeconomy becomes integral to sustainable urban development.

Urban Governance for the Bioeconomy

Urban governance is central to creating the conditions in which the bioeconomy can flourish. Cities are hubs of innovation, consumption, and resource flows, and they require governance frameworks that not only regulate activity but also encourage collaboration and experimentation. Effective governance ensures that the transition to bioeconomic systems is coherent, equitable, and aligned with broader sustainability objectives. Without appropriate governance, bioeconomic initiatives risk remaining fragmented or failing to scale in ways that deliver systemic change.

A key aspect of urban governance for the bioeconomy is the creation of supportive policy environments. Municipal authorities have the power to establish regulations, incentives, and standards that shape markets and influence behavior. Examples include mandates for waste separation, green procurement policies that prioritize bio-based materials, and zoning regulations that accommodate urban agriculture and biorefineries. By setting clear rules and incentives, city governments can reduce market uncertainty and provide the stability that investors and entrepreneurs require to develop bio-based industries.

Institutional coordination is another crucial element. The bioeconomy spans multiple sectors—energy, food, water, waste, transport, and housing—making siloed governance approaches ineffective. Urban governance must promote cross-departmental collaboration, ensuring that initiatives in one domain reinforce rather than undermine those in another. For example, integrating waste management with energy and water planning creates synergies that maximize the value of biological resources. Multi-level governance that connects municipal authorities with regional, national, and international institutions further strengthens alignment and enables cities to access broader funding and technical support.

Public participation is also fundamental. The bioeconomy is not simply a technological transition; it involves rethinking consumption patterns, lifestyles, and social practices. Citizens must be engaged in decision-making processes and empowered to participate in bioeconomic activities such as community composting, local food initiatives, and waste reduction programs. Governance frameworks that encourage inclusivity build trust, foster social acceptance, and ensure that the benefits of the bioeconomy are equitably distributed. Civic engagement also enhances accountability, helping governments and businesses remain responsive to community priorities.

Innovation governance plays a vital role in accelerating the bioeconomy in cities. Urban authorities can support research, development, and demonstration projects by providing testbeds, incubators, and funding mechanisms. By facilitating partnerships between universities, startups, and established companies, governance structures can help scale new bio-based technologies and business models. Cities that position themselves as centers of experimentation can attract talent, investment, and international recognition, further reinforcing their leadership in the global bioeconomy.

Finally, governance must ensure that urban bioeconomic transitions are just and sustainable. This includes embedding equity considerations into policies so that vulnerable groups are not excluded from the opportunities created by new industries. It also requires robust monitoring and evaluation systems to track progress, identify unintended consequences, and adapt policies over time. Transparency in governance processes builds confidence among stakeholders, while adaptive management allows cities to remain flexible in the face of rapid technological and social change.

Urban governance for the bioeconomy is therefore multifaceted, encompassing regulation, coordination, participation, innovation, and equity. When designed effectively, governance provides the foundation for cities to harness the full potential of biological resources and circular systems, turning urban areas into engines of sustainable transformation.

Policy Instruments to Promote Bioeconomic Transition

The transition to a bioeconomy requires more than technological innovation and entrepreneurial activity; it demands well-designed policy instruments that create enabling conditions, reduce risks, and encourage adoption. Policy instruments act as levers through which governments, particularly at the urban level, can stimulate investment, influence behavior, and align diverse stakeholders around sustainability goals. A balanced mix of regulatory, economic, and informational tools ensures that bioeconomic initiatives gain traction and scale effectively.

Regulatory instruments form the backbone of bioeconomic governance, providing clear rules that set minimum standards and shape market behavior. Examples include mandates for organic waste separation, bans on single-use plastics, and requirements for biodegradable or bio-based packaging in urban markets. Building codes can be adapted to encourage the use of bio-based construction materials, while zoning policies can make space for urban agriculture, green infrastructure, and biorefineries. By establishing binding requirements, regulatory instruments reduce ambiguity and create a level playing field, ensuring that all actors move toward more sustainable practices.

Economic instruments are equally critical in promoting the bioeconomy by influencing financial incentives. Subsidies, grants, and tax breaks can reduce the cost of adopting bio-based technologies and encourage businesses to invest in research and development. For example, municipalities can offer financial incentives for companies that utilize organic waste as feedstock for energy or materials. Conversely, taxes on fossil-based products and landfill disposal can discourage unsustainable practices, making bio-based alternatives more competitive. Green bonds and public-private investment funds provide additional channels to mobilize capital for large-scale bioeconomic projects, such as renewable energy infrastructure or urban food systems.

Market-based instruments complement these approaches by leveraging the power of supply and demand. Extended producer responsibility schemes require manufacturers to take responsibility for the end-of-life management of their products, incentivizing the design of biodegradable and recyclable goods. Public procurement policies that prioritize bio-based products create predictable demand, stimulating production and innovation. Certification schemes and eco-labeling further guide consumer choices, rewarding businesses that adopt bioeconomic practices with greater market visibility.

Informational and educational instruments strengthen the transition by raising awareness, building skills, and fostering cultural change. Public campaigns can encourage citizens to separate organic waste, reduce food waste, and adopt sustainable consumption patterns. Training programs and workforce development initiatives prepare employees for emerging roles in bio-based industries, ensuring that the labor market adapts to new opportunities. Knowledge-sharing platforms allow cities, businesses, and communities to learn from each other's experiences, accelerating the diffusion of successful models.

Innovation-focused instruments are particularly important in urban contexts, where experimentation and scaling are key. Governments can establish living labs, pilot projects, and demonstration zones where bioeconomic solutions are tested under real-world conditions.

Support for research and development through funding and partnerships with universities and private firms helps bring new technologies to market more quickly. By acting as conveners, municipalities can foster collaboration across sectors and disciplines, ensuring that bioeconomic transitions are not fragmented but integrated into broader urban sustainability agendas.

Policy instruments must also be adaptive. The bioeconomy is dynamic, shaped by rapid advances in biotechnology, changing market conditions, and evolving societal expectations. Instruments that are regularly evaluated and refined can remain effective as circumstances shift. A mix of strict regulations, supportive incentives, and participatory approaches ensures that the bioeconomic transition balances environmental objectives with economic growth and social equity.

In sum, policy instruments to promote the bioeconomy are diverse and interconnected, ranging from regulatory mandates to economic incentives and informational strategies. When deployed thoughtfully and in combination, they create an ecosystem in which cities can accelerate the transition toward circular, regenerative, and sustainable bioeconomic systems.

Role of International Frameworks and Agreements

International frameworks and agreements play a pivotal role in shaping the conditions under which the bioeconomy can emerge and thrive. Because the bioeconomy is deeply interconnected with global challenges such as climate change, biodiversity loss, food security, and sustainable development, international cooperation provides legitimacy, guidance, and coordination for local and national action. Urban centers, as key drivers of bioeconomic transformation, often align their strategies with these broader frameworks, ensuring consistency and unlocking opportunities for funding, partnerships, and innovation.

One of the most influential frameworks is the Paris Agreement under the United Nations Framework Convention on Climate Change. Its call for reducing greenhouse gas emissions and transitioning to low-carbon economies creates strong incentives for bioeconomic approaches that substitute fossil-based inputs with renewable biological resources. Bioenergy, bio-based materials, and circular waste-to-resource systems are all directly linked to climate mitigation. Cities that commit to aligning with Paris goals often find the bioeconomy a practical pathway for reducing emissions while also improving resilience and creating green jobs.

The Sustainable Development Goals (SDGs) provide another overarching framework, integrating environmental, social, and economic dimensions of sustainability. Several goals directly support bioeconomic principles, including responsible consumption and production (SDG 12), climate action (SDG 13), life on land (SDG 15), and life below water (SDG 14). The SDGs also emphasize partnerships and inclusivity, encouraging governments, businesses, and civil society to collaborate on transformative change. Urban bioeconomy initiatives—such as nutrient cycling, sustainable food systems, and circular material use—directly contribute to achieving multiple SDGs, making them attractive for international recognition and support.

The Convention on Biological Diversity (CBD) further strengthens the role of the bioeconomy by promoting the sustainable use of biodiversity and ecosystem services. Its Global Biodiversity Framework highlights the importance of conserving natural resources while enabling sustainable economic development. For cities, this means integrating green infrastructure, protecting urban biodiversity, and promoting nature-based solutions that align with bioeconomic principles. By embedding biodiversity goals into urban planning, municipalities ensure that bioeconomic initiatives support ecological integrity as well as economic prosperity.

Trade agreements and international standards also influence the development of the bioeconomy. Harmonized certification systems for bio-based products, such as eco-labels and sustainability standards, create trust and facilitate international markets. These frameworks reduce trade barriers for bio-based goods and provide consumers with confidence in the environmental claims of products. For urban industries, compliance with international standards allows them to access broader markets and attract investment, while consumers benefit from transparency and accountability.

In addition, international financial mechanisms such as the Green Climate Fund and the Global Environment Facility provide funding to support bioeconomic transitions, particularly in developing countries and cities facing resource constraints. By aligning with international agreements, cities can access grants, loans, and technical support to pilot and scale bioeconomic solutions. This financial support not only accelerates local projects but also integrates them into global efforts toward sustainability.

Overall, international frameworks and agreements provide the scaffolding upon which local and national bioeconomy strategies are built. They establish shared goals, create mechanisms for accountability, and mobilize resources that make ambitious action possible. For cities, aligning with these frameworks not only ensures consistency with global sustainability agendas but also opens opportunities for innovation, cooperation, and leadership in the transition toward bioeconomic futures.

Integrating Bioeconomy into National and Local Agendas

Integrating the bioeconomy into national and local agendas is essential for ensuring that the transition toward sustainable, circular systems is coherent, well-coordinated, and effective. The bioeconomy touches multiple sectors—agriculture, energy, waste management, manufacturing, and urban planning—making it a cross-cutting priority that cannot be pursued in isolation. Embedding bioeconomic principles into policy frameworks at all levels of governance aligns objectives, mobilizes resources, and facilitates collaboration among stakeholders.

At the national level, governments play a crucial role in setting strategic visions and long-term targets for the bioeconomy. National bioeconomy strategies define priorities, identify sectors for investment, and establish clear goals for reducing reliance on fossil-based resources. These strategies often align with international frameworks such as the Paris Agreement and the Sustainable Development Goals, ensuring consistency with global sustainability objectives. By providing a unifying vision, national agendas help avoid fragmented initiatives and encourage regional and municipal authorities to design policies that complement overarching goals.

Integrating the bioeconomy into national policy also requires embedding it within broader economic, environmental, and industrial frameworks. Climate action plans, circular economy roadmaps, and green growth strategies can all include bioeconomic components, ensuring that biological resources and circular processes become part of mainstream policy. By aligning energy policies with bioenergy targets, agricultural strategies with nutrient recycling, and industrial policies with bio-based material development, national agendas can create synergies that accelerate the transition. Cross-ministerial coordination is especially important to ensure consistency across departments responsible for energy, environment, agriculture, health, and industry.

At the local level, municipalities have the unique capacity to translate national visions into concrete actions. Urban areas generate large resource flows and waste streams, making them natural laboratories for bioeconomic innovation. Local governments can integrate bioeconomy principles into urban planning, zoning, procurement, and service delivery. For instance, municipal waste management strategies can prioritize organic waste valorization, while city infrastructure projects can favor bio-based construction materials. Local agendas are also critical for promoting community engagement, ensuring that residents understand, support, and participate in bioeconomic initiatives.

Integrating bioeconomy into local agendas often involves partnerships with businesses, universities, and civil society organizations. Cities can act as conveners, bringing stakeholders together to co-design policies and pilot new solutions. Local innovation ecosystems—such as incubators, living labs, and demonstration projects—benefit from municipal support and provide the testing ground for scaling bioeconomic technologies. By fostering local collaboration, municipalities ensure that the bioeconomy becomes not only a top-down mandate but also a bottom-up movement rooted in community participation and entrepreneurship.

Financing is another critical aspect of integration. National and local agendas must align funding mechanisms to support research, innovation, and implementation. National governments can provide large-scale grants, tax incentives, and green bonds, while municipalities can mobilize local budgets and public-private partnerships. Coordinated financing ensures that resources are directed toward priority areas and that both large-scale infrastructure and grassroots initiatives are supported.

Incorporating the bioeconomy into national and local agendas also requires monitoring and accountability. Indicators that track progress in resource efficiency, bio-based product use, emissions reductions, and job creation help ensure that policies remain on course. Transparent reporting enables policymakers to adapt strategies over time and build public trust in the transition process.

Integrating the bioeconomy into national and local agendas ensures that efforts are consistent, mutually reinforcing, and capable of delivering systemic change. National visions set the direction, while local actions bring bioeconomic principles to life in practical, tangible ways. This alignment creates the foundation for building resilient, circular, and sustainable societies.

Public-Private Partnerships for Bioeconomic Growth

Public-private partnerships (PPPs) are essential mechanisms for advancing the bioeconomy, particularly in urban contexts where the demand for innovation, infrastructure, and financing exceeds the capacity of any single actor. By bringing together the resources and expertise of governments, businesses, and civil society, PPPs provide a collaborative framework for designing, funding, and scaling bioeconomic initiatives. These partnerships help overcome barriers such as high upfront costs, technological risks, and limited public budgets while ensuring that projects are aligned with broader sustainability objectives.

One of the main advantages of PPPs in the bioeconomy is their ability to mobilize investment for large-scale projects. Bioeconomic infrastructure, including biorefineries, advanced waste-to-energy facilities, and bio-based construction systems, requires significant capital expenditures. Public actors often lack the financial capacity to deliver these alone, while private investors may hesitate without risk-sharing mechanisms. PPPs provide a balanced arrangement where governments de-risk projects through subsidies, guarantees, or regulatory support, encouraging private firms to commit capital and expertise. This collaboration accelerates the transition by ensuring that bioeconomic solutions are not confined to pilot projects but are implemented at scale.

PPPs also play a vital role in fostering innovation. Many bioeconomic technologies are still emerging, and their successful deployment requires joint efforts in research, development, and demonstration. Governments can support innovation by funding research institutions and offering tax incentives, while private companies contribute technical know-how, market access, and commercialization pathways. When these elements are combined, PPPs create ecosystems where new technologies can be tested, refined, and scaled in real-world urban environments. Pilot zones, innovation hubs, and demonstration districts are practical manifestations of such collaborations, showcasing the potential of bio-based solutions to broader audiences.

Another critical contribution of PPPs is their role in creating markets for bio-based products and services. Public authorities can leverage their purchasing power to stimulate demand for renewable construction materials, biodegradable packaging, or bio-based energy solutions. When procurement standards prioritize bio-based alternatives, private firms are incentivized to innovate and expand production. In return, businesses bring efficiencies, competitiveness, and consumer-oriented strategies that help scale these markets. This market-shaping function is particularly important in cities, where concentrated demand can rapidly accelerate adoption.

Governance and accountability are also strengthened through PPPs. By involving multiple stakeholders, PPPs distribute responsibilities, enhance transparency, and encourage collaborative decision-making. Citizens benefit from services that are more efficiently delivered, while businesses gain from predictable policy environments and clearer market signals. Mechanisms such as performance-based contracts ensure that both public and private partners remain committed to agreed sustainability targets. In this way, PPPs foster trust and long-term commitment, which are necessary for the systemic change that the bioeconomy requires.

Finally, PPPs help align local initiatives with national and international agendas. By coordinating with national governments and global frameworks, cities can ensure that their bioeconomic projects contribute to wider sustainability goals. PPPs thus serve as platforms that not only deliver local solutions but also reinforce global commitments, from climate mitigation to biodiversity protection.

Public-private partnerships are therefore powerful tools for advancing bioeconomic growth. By pooling resources, sharing risks, and co-creating solutions, they enable cities to bridge gaps between ambition and implementation, transforming the bioeconomy from a theoretical concept into a practical reality that delivers economic, social, and environmental benefits.

Chapter 3: Circular Bio-Based Industries

Circular bio-based industries are central to the urban bioeconomy, transforming the way cities produce, consume, and manage resources. By replacing fossil-based processes with renewable biological inputs and embedding circularity into production cycles, these industries create value while minimizing waste and environmental impacts. They operate across multiple sectors, including energy, construction, food, and materials, linking urban metabolism with regenerative economic models. This chapter examines the principles and practices of circular bio-based industries, highlighting how they close resource loops, foster innovation, and integrate with urban systems to build resilient, low-carbon, and sustainable city economies.

Bio-Based Materials and Urban Applications

Bio-based materials are central to advancing the urban bioeconomy, offering sustainable alternatives to fossil-derived and resource-intensive products traditionally used in construction, manufacturing, and consumer goods. These materials are derived from renewable biological resources such as wood, crops, algae, and organic waste, and they can be designed to be biodegradable, recyclable, or regenerative. Their integration into cities supports circularity, reduces carbon footprints, and contributes to healthier urban environments. With the rapid pace of urbanization, bio-based materials present a practical pathway to decarbonize infrastructure and create resilient, sustainable cities.

One of the most prominent applications of bio-based materials in urban contexts is in the construction sector. Buildings account for a significant portion of global greenhouse gas emissions, largely due to the production and use of conventional materials like concrete, steel, and plastics. Bio-based alternatives such as cross-laminated timber, hempcrete, bamboo, and mycelium-based composites provide renewable and low-carbon substitutes. These materials not only store carbon during their lifecycle but also offer durability, thermal efficiency, and design flexibility. Incorporating them into housing, commercial buildings, and public infrastructure reduces reliance on high-emission materials and supports the shift toward climate-neutral urban development.

Bio-based materials also play a role in packaging and consumer goods, which are significant sources of urban waste. Single-use plastics and non-biodegradable packaging create challenges for waste management systems and contribute to pollution. Alternatives such as bio-based plastics, starch-based films, and cellulose-derived packaging offer biodegradable or compostable solutions. By integrating these materials into urban markets, cities can reduce plastic pollution, ease pressure on landfills, and improve the circularity of consumer products. Municipal procurement policies and waste management systems can further reinforce their adoption by creating clear demand and efficient end-of-life processing pathways.

Textiles are another sector where bio-based materials have important urban applications. Traditional textile production is resource-intensive and heavily reliant on synthetic fibers derived from fossil fuels. Bio-based textiles made from organic cotton, hemp, bamboo, and even bioengineered fibers provide sustainable alternatives. In cities, where fashion and consumer culture drive high levels of consumption, promoting bio-based textiles can reduce environmental impacts and support circular urban economies. Clothing recycling programs, combined with innovation in biodegradable fibers, help close material loops in the textile industry.

Urban mobility and infrastructure also benefit from bio-based innovations. Biofuels derived from waste oils, algae, or crop residues can power public transportation systems, reducing dependence on fossil fuels. Additionally, bio-based composites and polymers are increasingly used in automotive and transport applications, offering lightweight, durable, and renewable alternatives to conventional materials. These developments contribute to decarbonizing urban mobility while supporting the bioeconomy's growth.

Beyond their environmental benefits, bio-based materials also contribute to public health and social well-being. Many conventional materials emit harmful pollutants during production or use, whereas bio-based alternatives often have lower toxicity and better indoor air quality outcomes. Green urban design that incorporates natural and bio-based elements—such as living walls, green roofs, and biodegradable insulation—creates healthier living environments and fosters stronger connections between urban populations and nature.

The adoption of bio-based materials in cities, however, requires supportive governance, innovation, and market development. Standards, certifications, and incentives are needed to ensure quality, safety, and scalability. Collaboration between public authorities, industry, and research institutions is essential for accelerating the development and deployment of new materials. By embedding bio-based solutions into urban systems, cities can become leaders in sustainability, demonstrating how renewable resources and circular processes can reshape infrastructure, consumption, and daily life.

Bio-based materials are therefore more than substitutes for conventional products—they are enablers of systemic transformation. Their urban applications illustrate how the bioeconomy can be embedded into everyday life, turning cities into living laboratories of circularity and sustainability.

Industrial Symbiosis and Urban Metabolism

Industrial symbiosis and urban metabolism are two interrelated concepts that lie at the heart of advancing the urban bioeconomy. Both emphasize how materials, energy, water, and byproducts flow through cities, and how these flows can be managed to create synergies rather than waste. By rethinking resource use in systemic and collaborative ways, cities can reduce environmental impacts, foster innovation, and strengthen economic resilience. Together, industrial symbiosis and urban metabolism provide the foundation for building circular urban systems where biological and industrial processes operate in harmony.

Urban metabolism refers to the study and management of the material and energy flows within a city, treating it as a living organism that consumes resources, generates outputs, and produces waste. Just as a biological organism metabolizes nutrients, cities metabolize water, food, energy, and raw materials. Traditional urban metabolism is often linear: resources enter, are consumed, and leave as waste. This model creates inefficiencies and environmental pressures. Transitioning to circular urban metabolism means reconfiguring systems so that waste streams are minimized and outputs are reintegrated as inputs. In this way, cities evolve into self-sustaining systems where biological and technical cycles are interconnected.

Industrial symbiosis applies this principle at the level of industries and businesses. It involves collaboration among companies and institutions to exchange resources such as energy, water, and byproducts. Waste from one sector becomes a valuable input for another, creating networks of mutual benefit. In urban areas, where industries, utilities, and service providers are often concentrated in close proximity, the potential for industrial symbiosis is especially high. For example, organic waste from food processing can be used in bioenergy production, while excess heat from manufacturing can supply district heating systems. Such exchanges reduce resource consumption, cut costs, and lower emissions.

The integration of industrial symbiosis into urban metabolism strengthens the circularity of cities. Wastewater treatment plants can recover nutrients and energy for agriculture and industry. Biorefineries can process organic municipal waste into fuels, chemicals, and fertilizers. Construction and demolition waste can be recycled into bio-based building materials, reducing demand for virgin resources. These interactions create cascading systems where resources are continually cycled, minimizing losses and maximizing value creation. By connecting industrial and biological cycles, urban areas transform from sites of extraction and disposal into regenerative ecosystems.

Governance plays a crucial role in enabling industrial symbiosis within urban metabolism. Municipal authorities can design policies and regulations that encourage resource sharing and penalize wasteful practices. Zoning laws can be adapted to co-locate complementary industries, while incentives such as tax reductions or grants can encourage businesses to participate in resource exchange networks. Publicly supported platforms that facilitate information sharing among companies help identify opportunities for collaboration, reducing the transaction costs and knowledge gaps that often hinder industrial symbiosis.

Social and economic benefits extend beyond resource efficiency. Industrial symbiosis fosters innovation, creating new business models and revenue streams. It supports local job creation in recycling, bio-based production, and urban farming. By reducing dependency on imported raw materials, cities enhance their economic resilience. Communities also benefit from improved air quality, reduced waste, and more sustainable urban infrastructure.

Industrial symbiosis and urban metabolism together demonstrate how cities can reconfigure their resource flows to align with the principles of the bioeconomy. By linking businesses, infrastructure, and ecosystems in dynamic exchanges, urban areas move closer to becoming regenerative, circular systems that support both economic development and environmental sustainability.

Valorization of Organic Waste in Cities

The valorization of organic waste is a cornerstone of the urban bioeconomy, transforming what was once seen as a burden into valuable resources that fuel circular systems. Cities generate large volumes of organic waste through households, food services, markets, and industries. Traditionally, much of this waste has been sent to landfills, incinerated, or left to decompose, creating environmental issues such as greenhouse gas emissions, leachate contamination, and inefficient use of nutrients. By adopting valorization strategies, urban areas can capture the inherent value in

34

organic materials, converting them into energy, fertilizers, and bio-based products while reducing environmental impacts.

One of the most common approaches to valorizing organic waste is energy recovery. Through anaerobic digestion, organic matter is broken down by microorganisms to produce biogas, which can be used for electricity generation, heating, or as a renewable substitute for natural gas. Cities that integrate anaerobic digestion into their waste management systems not only reduce landfill volumes but also contribute to energy security and carbon reduction goals. Composting provides another pathway for converting organic waste into nutrient-rich soil amendments, supporting urban agriculture, landscaping, and green infrastructure projects. These methods close nutrient loops and return essential resources to the environment.

Beyond energy and soil products, organic waste can serve as feedstock for biorefineries, which extract high-value compounds such as bio-based chemicals, plastics, and fuels. For example, food waste can be converted into lactic acid for biodegradable plastics, while agricultural residues can be processed into biofuels. The integration of urban biorefineries into city planning creates hubs of innovation that turn local waste streams into a diverse range of products, reducing dependence on fossil-derived inputs. This cascading use of organic materials ensures that they generate multiple layers of value before being reintegrated into natural cycles.

Valorization also contributes to more efficient and resilient food systems in cities. Food waste reduction and recovery initiatives ensure that edible food is diverted to people in need, while inedible fractions are directed to animal feed or industrial uses. These strategies reduce the social and environmental costs of food waste while improving the efficiency of urban food supply chains. At the same time, closing nutrient cycles through waste valorization supports sustainable agriculture by providing fertilizers derived from compost or digestate, reducing reliance on synthetic inputs.

Governance and infrastructure are crucial enablers of organic waste valorization. Municipalities must establish collection systems that separate organic waste at the source, preventing contamination that undermines the quality of recovered materials. Regulations and incentives can encourage businesses and households to participate in waste separation, while procurement policies can create demand for compost, biogas, and bio-based products. Partnerships between municipalities, private firms, and research institutions help develop the technology, investment, and market frameworks required to scale organic waste valorization initiatives.

Valorization also delivers social and economic benefits. It generates green jobs in waste collection, processing, and product development, while creating new opportunities for entrepreneurship in bio-based industries. Communities benefit from reduced environmental burdens, improved local energy supplies, and healthier urban environments. By reframing organic waste as a resource rather than a liability, cities strengthen their role as engines of circular innovation and sustainable growth.

The valorization of organic waste in cities is therefore more than a technical solution; it is a systemic approach that integrates waste management, energy, food systems, and industrial innovation. By unlocking the value of biological materials, cities can transform waste into a driver of sustainability, resilience, and economic opportunity.

Biorefineries as Urban Hubs

Biorefineries are emerging as critical components of the urban bioeconomy, serving as hubs that transform biological resources and organic waste into valuable products such as bioenergy, bio-based chemicals, materials, and fertilizers. In the context of cities, biorefineries embody the principle of circularity by closing resource loops and ensuring that organic materials are continuously repurposed rather than discarded. Their integration into urban systems supports waste management, reduces dependence on fossil-based resources, and stimulates local economic development.

Unlike traditional industrial facilities, biorefineries are designed to process diverse feedstocks, often sourced from urban waste streams. Municipal solid waste, food waste, wastewater sludge, and agricultural residues from peri-urban areas can all serve as inputs. By converting these materials into useful outputs, biorefineries reduce landfill use, mitigate greenhouse gas emissions, and turn environmental challenges into opportunities. For example, wastewater treatment plants can be expanded into urban biorefineries, recovering biogas, clean water, and nutrients, thereby transforming a waste facility into a resource center.

The strength of biorefineries lies in their ability to apply a cascading use approach to biomass. Feedstocks can first be processed into high-value products such as bioplastics or bio-based chemicals, and the remaining fractions can be converted into energy or fertilizers. This maximization of value mirrors natural ecosystems where resources are used repeatedly in multiple forms. In urban contexts, such cascading use ensures that organic waste contributes to both industrial processes and local environmental regeneration.

Biorefineries also serve as anchors for industrial symbiosis in cities. Their operations generate byproducts—such as heat, digestate, or carbon dioxide—that can be shared with nearby industries or urban infrastructure. Excess heat from biogas production can supply district heating networks, while digestate from anaerobic digestion can support urban agriculture. This integration with other urban systems enhances efficiency, reduces costs, and strengthens the resilience of local economies. By functioning as nodes in broader resource-sharing networks, biorefineries transform urban metabolism into a circular system.

Governance and planning play a decisive role in positioning biorefineries as urban hubs. Municipalities can create enabling environments through zoning regulations, public procurement policies, and incentives for bio-based products. Partnerships between city authorities, private firms, and research institutions can mobilize investment and innovation, ensuring that biorefineries meet both economic and sustainability goals. Public support is also important, as successful projects often rely on citizen participation in waste separation and local acceptance of new facilities. Transparent communication about environmental and social benefits can build trust and strengthen community engagement.

Beyond environmental benefits, biorefineries generate economic and social value. They create green jobs in technology development, facility operation, logistics, and product distribution. They also foster entrepreneurship by enabling small and medium-sized enterprises to develop new bio-based products for urban markets. Educational institutions can collaborate with biorefineries to train workers and conduct applied research, further embedding bioeconomic innovation into the fabric of the city.

Biorefineries as urban hubs demonstrate how cities can become leaders in bioeconomic transformation. By turning waste streams into resources, connecting with other industries through symbiosis, and driving innovation in bio-based products, they provide a practical pathway toward circular and regenerative urban economies. Their role as anchors of the urban bioeconomy underscores the potential for cities to harness biology and technology in building sustainable futures.

Urban Manufacturing and Resource Efficiency

Urban manufacturing is undergoing a transformation as cities embrace the principles of the bioeconomy and circularity. Traditionally, manufacturing has been resource-intensive, generating significant waste, emissions, and reliance on fossil-based materials. In urban contexts, where space is limited and resource flows are concentrated, the inefficiencies of linear manufacturing systems become especially visible. The integration of resource efficiency into urban manufacturing reimagines production as part of a circular economy, where materials are conserved, waste is minimized, and biological resources are valorized.

One of the central opportunities for improving urban manufacturing lies in the adoption of bio-based inputs. Replacing conventional materials with bio-based alternatives reduces the carbon footprint of production and lessens dependence on finite resources. For example, bio-based plastics, textiles, and composites derived from renewable biomass can substitute fossil-derived products in consumer goods and packaging. Incorporating locally sourced bio-based materials also shortens supply chains, lowering transportation emissions and increasing resilience against global market fluctuations. This shift aligns urban manufacturing with the broader goals of the bioeconomy by embedding biological cycles into industrial processes.

Resource efficiency is another critical dimension of reconfiguring urban manufacturing. Efficiency is achieved through strategies such as energy optimization, water reuse, and waste reduction. Closed-loop systems allow materials to be recovered and reintegrated into production cycles, reducing demand for virgin resources. Additive manufacturing, or 3D printing, provides opportunities to design products with minimal material use and enables localized production, which decreases waste and transportation requirements. Smart technologies, including sensors and data analytics, can monitor resource flows in real time, helping factories identify inefficiencies and implement corrective measures.

Industrial symbiosis complements these approaches by linking manufacturing facilities with other urban systems. Waste heat, water, and byproducts from one manufacturer can serve as resources for another, creating networks of exchange that enhance efficiency across the city. For example, surplus organic residues from food processing plants can be directed to bioenergy facilities, while waste materials from construction can be recycled into new bio-based building products. These synergies demonstrate how urban manufacturing can be embedded into the larger metabolism of the city, supporting circularity and minimizing waste.

Governance and policy frameworks play a pivotal role in advancing resource efficiency in urban manufacturing. Municipalities can support the transition by offering incentives for energy efficiency upgrades, waste valorization technologies, and adoption of bio-based materials. Urban planning can allocate space for eco-industrial parks, where manufacturers are co-located to maximize opportunities for resource sharing. Regulations requiring waste separation, recycling, and emissions reductions further reinforce circular practices. Public procurement policies that favor bio-based and resource-efficient products create demand and encourage businesses to innovate.

Urban manufacturing that prioritizes resource efficiency also delivers economic and social benefits. By reducing input costs, companies improve competitiveness, while investments in green technologies create jobs and stimulate local innovation. Consumers benefit from sustainable products and cleaner urban environments, while cities enhance their resilience by reducing dependency on global resource flows. Collaboration between governments, industries, and communities ensures that the benefits of resource-efficient manufacturing are widely shared.

Urban manufacturing integrated with resource efficiency principles exemplifies how cities can lead the transition to bioeconomic systems. By combining bio-based inputs, circular production strategies, and symbiotic networks, cities transform manufacturing into a driver of sustainability. This shift positions urban centers as pioneers of regenerative industry, turning the challenges of resource scarcity and environmental pressure into opportunities for innovation and resilience.

Chapter 4: Sustainable Urban Infrastructure

Sustainable urban infrastructure provides the physical and organizational foundation for embedding bioeconomic principles into cities. Traditional infrastructure systems—roads, buildings, water networks, and energy grids—have often been designed around linear models that prioritize short-term efficiency over long-term resilience. In contrast, sustainable infrastructure emphasizes circularity, resource efficiency, and ecological integration. It connects transportation, energy, water, and waste systems in ways that regenerate resources rather than deplete them. This chapter explores how sustainable urban infrastructure can support the bioeconomy by aligning design, construction, and operation with renewable inputs, ecosystem services, and innovative technologies that drive resilient urban development.

Green Infrastructure and Urban Ecosystems

Green infrastructure and urban ecosystems are central to embedding bioeconomy principles into cities, providing natural solutions that enhance resilience, resource efficiency, and human well-being. Unlike conventional infrastructure that often relies on resource-intensive, fossil-based materials, green infrastructure uses natural systems—trees, wetlands, parks, and green roofs—to deliver essential services such as air purification, stormwater management, and climate regulation. Urban ecosystems, when restored and integrated into planning, support biodiversity and create the ecological foundation on which sustainable cities can thrive.

One of the most significant contributions of green infrastructure is its role in managing water in cities. Traditional stormwater systems often treat rainfall as a waste product to be channeled away quickly, leading to flooding, pollution, and infrastructure stress. In contrast, green infrastructure captures, filters, and reuses water through features such as permeable pavements, bioswales, wetlands, and green roofs. These systems mimic natural hydrological cycles, reducing urban flooding, recharging groundwater, and improving water quality. By integrating green infrastructure into urban planning, cities can align water management with bioeconomic principles of circularity and regeneration.

Urban ecosystems also enhance air quality and mitigate climate change. Trees and vegetation absorb carbon dioxide and pollutants while providing shade that lowers urban heat island effects. By cooling city environments, green infrastructure reduces energy demand for air conditioning, thereby lowering emissions from power generation. Parks, green corridors, and urban forests not only deliver environmental benefits but also contribute to public health by offering spaces for recreation and reducing exposure to extreme heat. These ecological services are vital assets for cities seeking to reduce their ecological footprint while improving quality of life.

The integration of biodiversity into urban systems is another critical dimension of green infrastructure. Natural habitats are often fragmented by urbanization, but strategically designed green spaces can reconnect ecosystems, creating corridors for species and enhancing ecological resilience. Biodiverse urban environments are more robust in the face of climate extremes and provide a range of services, from pollination to soil regeneration. By protecting and restoring ecosystems within cities, urban planners can ensure that bioeconomic strategies support both human and ecological communities.

From an economic perspective, investing in green infrastructure is cost-effective over the long term. While initial investments may be higher than traditional infrastructure, the multiple benefits—reduced healthcare costs, avoided flood damage, lower energy bills, and enhanced property values—outweigh the costs. Moreover, green infrastructure generates jobs in design, maintenance, and ecological restoration, aligning with the bioeconomy's goal of creating sustainable employment opportunities. These co-benefits make green infrastructure an attractive policy option for cities seeking to balance environmental and economic objectives.

Social inclusion is also strengthened through green infrastructure. Access to urban nature improves mental and physical health, fosters social cohesion, and reduces inequality by providing shared public spaces. Community-based initiatives, such as neighborhood gardens and local restoration projects, empower residents to take part in shaping their environment and contribute to the local bioeconomy.

Green infrastructure and urban ecosystems thus exemplify how nature can be integrated into the design and function of cities. By restoring ecological processes, enhancing resilience, and delivering multiple benefits simultaneously, they transform urban environments into regenerative systems. Their role in the urban bioeconomy is indispensable, as they provide the foundation upon which circular, sustainable, and inclusive cities can be built.

Water-Sensitive Urban Design

Water-sensitive urban design (WSUD) is a holistic approach to city planning and infrastructure that integrates the management of water, urban development, and ecosystems. It seeks to ensure that urban growth aligns with natural hydrological processes, promoting sustainability, resilience, and quality of life. Unlike conventional systems that treat water primarily as a supply or waste issue, WSUD views water as a resource that flows through interconnected cycles of capture, use, treatment, and reuse. This perspective makes it a key element of the urban bioeconomy, embedding circularity and ecosystem thinking into city development.

A central principle of WSUD is the management of stormwater as a resource rather than a nuisance. Traditional urban drainage systems are designed to move rainwater away from streets and buildings as quickly as possible, often resulting in flooding, pollution of waterways, and the loss of valuable freshwater. WSUD strategies such as permeable pavements, rain gardens, bioswales, and wetlands allow stormwater to infiltrate into the ground, recharge aquifers, and be filtered naturally. These systems mimic natural hydrology, reducing flood risk while improving water quality and enhancing local biodiversity.

WSUD also emphasizes the integration of water reuse and recycling into urban systems. Greywater from households and stormwater collected from rooftops can be treated and reused for non-potable purposes such as irrigation, toilet flushing, or cooling. By diversifying water sources, cities reduce pressure on centralized supply systems and improve resilience against drought and climate variability. Decentralized water systems, often supported by WSUD, reduce energy demand for pumping and treatment while fostering localized circular water cycles.

Urban heat mitigation is another important benefit of WSUD. Water-sensitive features such as ponds, wetlands, and vegetated stormwater systems provide cooling effects that reduce the urban heat island phenomenon. By lowering surrounding air temperatures, these designs contribute to energy savings, improve comfort for residents, and reduce health risks associated with extreme heat. When combined with vegetation, WSUD systems create microclimates that enhance both environmental and social well-being.

The social dimension of WSUD is equally significant. Public spaces designed with water-sensitive features provide recreational, cultural, and aesthetic benefits. Parks, waterfronts, and community gardens that integrate water management become attractive places for residents, fostering stronger connections between people and their environment. WSUD also encourages citizen participation, as communities engage in maintaining green spaces, monitoring water quality, and advocating for sustainable water use. This inclusion strengthens urban resilience by aligning social and ecological priorities.

Governance frameworks and policy instruments are essential for mainstreaming WSUD. Municipal authorities can support its adoption through building codes, zoning regulations, and incentives for developers to incorporate water-sensitive features. Collaboration between planners, engineers, ecologists, and communities ensures that designs meet multiple objectives, from flood control to biodiversity enhancement. Financing mechanisms such as green infrastructure funds and public-private partnerships further enable the scaling of WSUD projects across cities.

Water-sensitive urban design demonstrates how integrating natural processes into infrastructure can transform the way cities manage resources. By aligning hydrological cycles with urban planning, WSUD provides solutions that reduce risks, conserve water, enhance ecosystems, and improve quality of life. Its principles illustrate the potential of the urban bioeconomy to create regenerative, resilient, and inclusive cities that thrive within ecological limits.

Bio-Based Building Materials and Construction Practices

The construction sector is one of the largest consumers of raw materials and producers of greenhouse gas emissions worldwide. Traditional building materials such as steel, cement, and plastics are energy-intensive to produce and have long-term environmental consequences. In response, cities are increasingly turning to bio-based materials and sustainable construction practices as part of the broader urban bioeconomy. By using renewable biological resources and circular design principles, bio-based building materials offer opportunities to decarbonize the built environment, reduce waste, and create healthier urban spaces.

One of the most widely adopted bio-based materials in construction is timber, particularly engineered forms such as cross-laminated timber and glue-laminated beams. These products combine strength and durability with the ability to sequester carbon throughout their lifecycle. Unlike steel or concrete, which release large amounts of carbon dioxide during production, timber stores carbon absorbed during tree growth. When sourced from sustainably managed forests, timber provides a renewable and low-carbon option for buildings of all scales, including multi-story urban developments.

45

Other innovative materials are emerging alongside timber. Hempcrete, made from hemp fibers mixed with lime, offers excellent insulation properties, is lightweight, and naturally regulates indoor humidity. Bamboo, with its rapid growth cycle and high tensile strength, provides another renewable option for structural and decorative applications. Mycelium-based composites, derived from fungal growth, can be molded into panels and bricks that are biodegradable and fire-resistant. These materials not only reduce reliance on fossil-based products but also open new possibilities for design and innovation in urban construction.

In addition to new materials, sustainable construction practices are central to the bioeconomy. Designing buildings for disassembly ensures that materials can be recovered and reused at the end of their lifecycle, supporting circularity. Modular construction techniques minimize waste by using prefabricated components that can be assembled efficiently on-site. Life-cycle assessment tools help architects and engineers evaluate the environmental impacts of materials and select options that align with sustainability goals. Together, these practices reduce resource consumption while enhancing the adaptability of urban infrastructure.

Bio-based materials also contribute to healthier living environments. Many conventional materials emit volatile organic compounds or create heat-trapping surfaces that exacerbate urban heat islands. In contrast, bio-based materials often improve indoor air quality, regulate temperature and moisture, and reduce energy demand for heating and cooling. Integrating green walls, bio-composites, and natural insulation into buildings strengthens the connection between urban residents and natural systems while supporting climate resilience.

Governance and market development are crucial for scaling bio-based construction. Standards and certification systems provide assurance of quality and sustainability, encouraging adoption by developers and builders. Public procurement policies that favor renewable materials can stimulate demand and create stable markets. Research and innovation funding supports the advancement of new materials and techniques, while education and training prepare professionals to work with bio-based alternatives. Municipalities, as regulators and major infrastructure developers, have a key role in setting targets for bio-based construction and demonstrating leadership through public projects.

The adoption of bio-based building materials and sustainable practices reflects a fundamental shift in how cities approach construction. Rather than relying on extractive and high-emission industries, the built environment becomes a driver of circularity, carbon sequestration, and ecological integration. By embedding bioeconomy principles into urban development, cities can create structures that not only meet human needs but also regenerate resources and contribute to long-term sustainability.

Smart Waste and Resource Management Systems

Smart waste and resource management systems are transforming the way cities handle materials, integrating digital technologies, data-driven decision-making, and circular economy principles to improve efficiency and sustainability. As urban populations grow, the volume of waste generated increases, creating significant pressures on landfills, incinerators, and municipal budgets. Traditional waste systems are often reactive and linear, focusing on disposal rather than prevention, recovery, or reuse. By embedding smart technologies into waste and resource management, cities can optimize collection, enhance recycling, and unlock the value of discarded materials, making them key drivers of the urban bioeconomy.

A central feature of smart waste management is the use of sensors and digital platforms to monitor waste generation and collection in real time. Smart bins equipped with fill-level sensors transmit data to waste collection operators, enabling dynamic routing of trucks and reducing unnecessary trips. This approach cuts fuel use, lowers emissions, and reduces costs while ensuring timely service. Data collected from these systems also provides insights into consumption patterns, helping municipalities and businesses design policies and initiatives to minimize waste at the source.

Resource recovery is another vital component. Smart systems improve sorting efficiency, ensuring that recyclables and organics are separated effectively from general waste. Automated facilities use robotics, machine learning, and optical recognition to identify and sort materials with precision, increasing recovery rates for plastics, metals, and organic matter. Organic fractions can then be directed to composting facilities or anaerobic digestion plants, producing fertilizers and biogas that contribute to circular urban economies. By leveraging technology, cities can reduce contamination in recycling streams, improving the quality of recovered materials and strengthening secondary markets.

Citizen engagement is critical to the success of smart waste and resource systems. Digital applications and platforms allow residents to track their waste generation, receive reminders about collection schedules, and learn how to properly sort materials. Gamification tools, such as rewards for recycling or penalties for non-compliance, encourage behavioral change and foster a culture of responsibility. Transparent feedback loops build public trust by showing residents how their efforts contribute to reducing waste and creating value in the bioeconomy.

Integration with broader urban systems further enhances the impact of smart waste management. For example, linking waste data with energy systems allows biogas production from organic waste to be optimized for local electricity or heating grids. Similarly, connecting recycling data with manufacturing sectors supports the supply of secondary raw materials for bio-based products. These linkages reflect the principles of urban metabolism, where waste streams are viewed as resources that circulate through interconnected urban systems.

Governance frameworks and policy instruments play a supportive role in advancing smart waste systems. Cities can establish regulations that mandate waste separation, set recycling targets, and provide incentives for businesses that adopt circular practices. Public-private partnerships help fund and operate smart waste infrastructure, combining municipal oversight with private-sector innovation. Investment in digital infrastructure, such as Internet of Things networks and data platforms, ensures that waste systems are scalable and adaptable to future demands.

Smart waste and resource management systems embody the shift from linear disposal models to circular, regenerative urban systems. By combining digital technology, resource recovery, and citizen participation, they enable cities to manage waste more efficiently while creating economic, environmental, and social value. Their integration into urban planning represents a significant step toward resilient and sustainable bioeconomic futures.

Integrating Bioeconomy in Urban Master Planning

Urban master planning provides the blueprint for how cities grow, function, and evolve, making it a crucial tool for embedding bioeconomy principles into urban systems. By integrating biological resources, circularity, and regenerative design into long-term planning, cities can transition from fossil-dependent, linear models toward resilient and sustainable systems. The bioeconomy emphasizes the use of renewable materials, waste valorization, and ecosystem services, all of which can be woven into the spatial, economic, and social dimensions of urban master plans.

One of the first steps in integrating the bioeconomy into master planning is rethinking resource flows as interconnected cycles rather than linear chains. Traditional planning often separates waste, energy, water, and food systems into distinct sectors, which limits opportunities for synergy. A bioeconomy-informed approach views these systems as interdependent, where outputs from one sector can serve as inputs for another. For instance, organic waste can be valorized into bioenergy or fertilizers, stormwater can be harvested and reused, and green spaces can be designed to deliver ecosystem services such as cooling and air purification. Embedding these principles into master plans ensures that cities are designed with circularity as a foundation.

Spatial planning is another critical area where the bioeconomy can be integrated. Land-use policies can prioritize the development of green infrastructure, urban agriculture, and biorefineries, embedding bioeconomic activities into the physical fabric of the city. Mixed-use zoning that co-locates residential, commercial, and industrial areas can support industrial symbiosis, where waste and byproducts are shared across sectors. Green corridors and multifunctional landscapes can connect ecosystems while providing social and economic benefits. By aligning spatial design with bioeconomic goals, master plans ensure that the urban form supports circular and regenerative practices.

Economic development strategies within master planning also offer avenues to promote the bioeconomy. Cities can designate innovation districts that focus on bio-based industries, providing hubs for research, entrepreneurship, and investment. Public procurement policies embedded in master plans can stimulate demand for bio-based materials in construction, packaging, and energy. Workforce training and education programs can be planned alongside economic initiatives, ensuring that citizens are equipped with the skills required to participate in emerging bio-based sectors. By aligning land use, infrastructure, and economic policy, master plans become instruments for advancing bioeconomic growth.

Social inclusion must also be emphasized in bioeconomy-oriented master planning. Communities need to be engaged in decision-making processes to ensure that bioeconomic initiatives address local needs and do not exacerbate inequality. Access to green spaces, affordable housing constructed with bio-based materials, and community composting or gardening initiatives are examples of how planning can align social equity with environmental sustainability. Incorporating citizen participation into the planning process builds ownership and strengthens the cultural foundations of the bioeconomy.

Governance and monitoring mechanisms embedded in master plans are vital for ensuring long-term success. Cities can set measurable targets for bioeconomic outcomes such as resource efficiency, waste diversion, and bio-based product adoption. Periodic reviews allow for adaptive management, ensuring that plans remain relevant in the face of technological, economic, or climate changes. Partnerships between municipalities, private firms, universities, and communities can be formalized through planning frameworks, ensuring coordinated implementation.

Integrating the bioeconomy in urban master planning thus redefines how cities envision their future. By embedding circularity, renewable resource use, and ecological integration into spatial and economic design, master plans become instruments for systemic transformation. This approach positions cities as leaders of sustainable development, capable of aligning human activity with the regenerative logic of nature.

Chapter 5: Food and Water Systems in the Bioeconomy

Food and water systems are at the heart of the urban bioeconomy, shaping how cities nourish populations while managing critical natural resources. Conventional approaches to food and water rely heavily on linear models of extraction, consumption, and disposal, leading to inefficiencies, pollution, and vulnerability to climate and economic shocks. The bioeconomy reframes these systems through circularity, nutrient recovery, and sustainable production, emphasizing resilience and resource regeneration. This chapter examines how cities can integrate bio-based practices into food and water systems, linking production, distribution, and reuse to create secure, efficient, and regenerative urban resource cycles.

Urban Agriculture and Bio-Based Food Systems

Urban agriculture and bio-based food systems are essential components of the urban bioeconomy, addressing the growing challenges of food security, resource efficiency, and sustainability in cities. With urban populations expanding rapidly, demand for food is rising while the ecological footprint of food production and distribution increases. Urban agriculture offers localized solutions by producing food closer to consumers, reducing transport emissions, and integrating food systems into the fabric of cities. Bio-based food systems expand this approach, incorporating biological resources, circularity, and innovation to create more sustainable and resilient urban food networks.

A key dimension of urban agriculture is its ability to repurpose underutilized urban spaces for food production. Rooftops, vertical farms, community gardens, and peri-urban land can all serve as sites for growing fruits, vegetables, and even proteins. These initiatives not only contribute to local food supply but also enhance urban biodiversity, reduce heat island effects, and provide recreational and educational opportunities. By embedding food production within the built environment, cities align consumption with local ecological cycles, a core principle of the bioeconomy.

Bio-based food systems extend beyond production to encompass the entire cycle of food resources, from inputs to waste management. Nutrient recovery from organic waste streams and wastewater provides sustainable fertilizers that replace synthetic alternatives. Innovations such as aquaponics and hydroponics integrate biological processes to produce food efficiently with reduced land, water, and chemical use. These systems are highly adaptable to urban environments where space and resources are constrained. By closing nutrient and water loops, bio-based food systems reduce environmental pressures while improving productivity.

Urban agriculture and bio-based systems also support more resilient food networks. Global supply chains are vulnerable to disruptions from climate change, economic instability, and geopolitical tensions. By producing food locally and integrating biological cycles into urban planning, cities can buffer themselves against external shocks. Shorter supply chains also mean fresher produce, lower spoilage rates, and reduced reliance on energy-intensive storage and transportation. In this way, urban food systems enhance both environmental sustainability and food security.

The social dimension of urban agriculture and bio-based food systems is equally significant. Community gardens and cooperative food initiatives foster social cohesion, provide opportunities for education, and promote healthier diets. Access to locally grown food reduces inequalities by making fresh produce more available in underserved neighborhoods. Employment opportunities also arise in bio-based food industries, from urban farming to food processing and waste valorization, contributing to inclusive economic development.

Governance and policy play a critical role in advancing urban agriculture and bio-based food systems. Zoning laws, subsidies, and procurement policies can incentivize the use of bio-based inputs, encourage rooftop or vertical farming, and support the integration of nutrient recovery into municipal services. Partnerships between local governments, businesses, and research institutions foster innovation and scale. Public awareness campaigns and education programs help build cultural acceptance of bio-based diets and urban farming practices.

Urban agriculture and bio-based food systems thus embody the principles of circularity, regeneration, and resilience at the core of the bioeconomy. By linking food production, consumption, and resource recovery within cities, they transform urban areas into active participants in sustainable food cycles. These systems not only reduce environmental pressures but also strengthen community ties and enhance the overall quality of life in urban environments.

Nutrient Cycling and Food-Water-Energy Nexus

Nutrient cycling and the food-water-energy (FWE) nexus are tightly interwoven elements of the urban bioeconomy, offering a framework to manage resources efficiently and regenerate ecological processes. Cities consume vast quantities of food, water, and energy while producing large amounts of waste. By integrating nutrient cycling into the FWE nexus, urban areas can close loops, reduce dependence on external inputs, and transform waste streams into valuable resources. This interconnected approach strengthens resilience, lowers environmental impacts, and enhances the sustainability of urban systems.

Nutrient cycling refers to the recovery and reuse of essential elements such as nitrogen, phosphorus, and carbon that sustain life. In conventional urban systems, these nutrients are often lost through food waste, wastewater, and runoff, contributing to environmental problems such as eutrophication, greenhouse gas emissions, and soil degradation. Circular approaches reclaim nutrients from organic waste and wastewater and reintegrate them into agriculture and industry. Composting, anaerobic digestion, and advanced treatment technologies convert waste into fertilizers, soil amendments, or biogas, ensuring that nutrients circulate rather than being discarded.

The food system is central to this cycle. Urban food production, whether through community gardens, vertical farming, or peri-urban agriculture, depends on reliable nutrient inputs. By redirecting organic waste and recovered nutrients back into food production, cities can reduce reliance on synthetic fertilizers and enhance soil health. This integration not only supports sustainable food supply chains but also reduces the environmental burden of agriculture. Nutrient cycling creates a feedback loop where urban consumption and waste management contribute directly to local food security.

Water is another critical component of the nexus. Traditional urban water management often treats wastewater as a disposal problem, but within a circular bioeconomy it becomes a source of nutrients, clean water, and energy. Nutrient recovery technologies in wastewater treatment plants capture phosphorus and nitrogen for use as fertilizers, while treated water can be reused for irrigation or industrial purposes. Coupling nutrient recovery with water reuse strengthens the resilience of cities against drought and reduces pollution of rivers and coastal ecosystems.

Energy links to both food and water systems through nutrient cycling. Organic waste and wastewater serve as feedstocks for anaerobic digestion, producing biogas that can replace fossil fuels in heating, electricity, or transport. Energy recovered from these systems reduces greenhouse gas emissions while providing decentralized power sources for cities. At the same time, the energy demands of food production and water treatment can be offset by bioenergy generated from urban nutrient flows, reinforcing synergies within the nexus.

Governance plays a critical role in aligning nutrient cycling with the FWE nexus. Policies that support waste segregation, incentivize nutrient recovery technologies, and integrate circularity into food and water systems are essential. Collaboration among utilities, farmers, businesses, and communities ensures that recovered nutrients are effectively reintegrated into local economies. Education and awareness campaigns also encourage residents to participate in waste separation and adopt sustainable consumption habits, reinforcing nutrient loops at the household level.

Nutrient cycling within the food-water-energy nexus exemplifies how cities can rethink resource use through bioeconomic principles. By connecting the flows of food, water, and energy, and by ensuring that nutrients circulate continuously, urban systems become more efficient, resilient, and regenerative. This integrated perspective turns resource challenges into opportunities for innovation and sustainability, advancing the broader vision of the urban bioeconomy.

Water Reuse and Bioeconomy Integration

Water reuse is a critical pillar of the urban bioeconomy, enabling cities to conserve resources, reduce environmental pressures, and create circular water systems that align with biological and regenerative principles. Traditionally, urban water management has operated on a linear model: freshwater is extracted, used once, treated as wastewater, and discharged into rivers, lakes, or oceans. This approach not only wastes valuable water but also loses the nutrients and energy embedded within it. Integrating water reuse into the bioeconomy transforms this linear model into a circular one, where wastewater becomes a resource that fuels new economic and ecological opportunities.

At the core of water reuse is the concept of closing loops within urban systems. Wastewater can be treated to different quality standards, allowing it to serve diverse purposes such as irrigation, industrial processes, or groundwater recharge. High-quality reclaimed water can even be used for potable purposes when advanced treatment technologies are applied. By reusing water locally, cities reduce their reliance on freshwater sources, many of which are under growing stress from climate change and population growth. This integration strengthens resilience while aligning with the bioeconomy's focus on renewable and regenerative resource use.

Beyond conserving water, reuse initiatives capture nutrients and energy embedded in wastewater. Nutrient recovery technologies extract phosphorus and nitrogen, which can be turned into fertilizers and reintegrated into urban and peri-urban agriculture. Anaerobic digestion of wastewater sludge produces biogas, contributing renewable energy to city grids. Heat recovery from wastewater streams provides additional opportunities for reducing fossil fuel use. These processes embody bioeconomic principles by transforming waste into valuable inputs for food, energy, and industrial systems, creating synergies across multiple sectors.

Water reuse also plays a key role in creating synergies between the food, water, and energy nexus. Reclaimed water supports urban agriculture and green infrastructure, reducing demand on freshwater supplies while providing reliable irrigation. Nutrients recovered from wastewater close loops between consumption and production, reducing the environmental impact of synthetic fertilizers. Energy produced through biogas recovery offsets the power required for water treatment, lowering overall carbon emissions. By linking these cycles, water reuse strengthens circularity and resilience in cities, making them better prepared for resource constraints and climate challenges.

Policy and governance are critical for scaling water reuse in the bioeconomy. Regulations that establish quality standards, incentives for reuse infrastructure, and public procurement policies create an enabling environment. Urban master plans that integrate water reuse into housing, industry, and green infrastructure ensure long-term alignment with bioeconomic goals. Public acceptance is equally important, as perceptions about the safety of reused water can either hinder or accelerate adoption. Awareness campaigns, education programs, and transparent communication about the benefits and safety of reclaimed water build trust and encourage participation.

Water reuse, when integrated into the bioeconomy, redefines how cities value and manage one of their most essential resources. Instead of being discarded, wastewater becomes a source of water, nutrients, and energy that supports circular and regenerative systems. This integration not only reduces environmental pressures but also creates economic opportunities, enhances resilience, and strengthens the ecological foundation of sustainable urban living.

Sustainable Diets and Urban Consumption Patterns

Sustainable diets and urban consumption patterns are critical components of the urban bioeconomy, shaping the way resources are used and determining the environmental footprint of cities. As urban populations grow, the demand for food, energy, and consumer goods increases, often leading to overconsumption and waste. The transition to sustainable diets and more responsible consumption behaviors not only reduces pressure on ecosystems but also supports the development of bio-based industries and circular resource flows. Cities, as hubs of innovation and lifestyle trends, have a unique capacity to drive these shifts and influence wider societal change.

A sustainable diet is one that meets nutritional needs while minimizing environmental impacts. It emphasizes diversity, seasonal and locally produced foods, and a reduced reliance on resource-intensive products such as red meat and ultra-processed goods. In urban contexts, diets rich in plant-based foods, sustainably sourced proteins, and bio-based alternatives contribute to lower greenhouse gas emissions, reduced water demand, and improved public health. Shifting urban food demand toward such diets creates opportunities for urban agriculture, vertical farming, and bio-based food industries that align with the bioeconomy.

Consumption patterns extend beyond food, encompassing the way urban residents purchase, use, and dispose of products. Cities are often characterized by high levels of consumption, with short product life cycles and significant volumes of waste. Integrating bioeconomy principles into consumption patterns involves prioritizing products made from renewable resources, choosing durable and repairable items, and supporting businesses that follow circular production models. For example, opting for packaging made from biodegradable materials or textiles derived from bio-based fibers reduces reliance on fossil-based inputs and lowers the environmental burden of consumer choices.

Urban infrastructure and governance play a decisive role in shaping these behaviors. Public procurement policies can set examples by sourcing bio-based food, materials, and services for schools, hospitals, and municipal facilities. Incentives for retailers and restaurants to offer sustainable food options expand consumer access to healthier and lower-impact diets. Educational campaigns and labeling systems that highlight the environmental footprint of products empower citizens to make informed choices. By creating supportive environments, cities can accelerate cultural shifts toward sustainable consumption.

Social and cultural dimensions are also significant in shaping sustainable diets and consumption patterns. Food and consumer practices are influenced by habits, traditions, and social norms, which can be leveraged to promote bioeconomic alternatives. Community initiatives such as farmers' markets, cooperative grocery stores, and food-sharing networks build local resilience and strengthen trust in sustainable practices. Social innovation, including sharing platforms and repair cafés, encourages collaborative consumption, reducing the demand for new resource-intensive products. These initiatives not only lower environmental impacts but also foster inclusivity and community cohesion.

Technology supports these transitions by providing tools for transparency and efficiency. Digital platforms connect consumers to local food producers, enabling direct purchase of seasonal and bio-based products. Apps that track consumption footprints help residents understand and reduce their impact, while blockchain systems ensure traceability of sustainable goods. These innovations make it easier for urban populations to align daily consumption with bioeconomic principles.

Sustainable diets and responsible consumption patterns in cities illustrate how individual choices and systemic frameworks converge to drive the bioeconomy. By fostering plant-based diets, reducing waste, supporting bio-based products, and promoting cultural change, cities can reduce their ecological footprint while creating healthier, more resilient communities. These changes are essential for embedding the bioeconomy into everyday urban life and achieving long-term sustainability.

Resilient Urban Food Supply Chains

Resilient urban food supply chains are vital for ensuring food security, reducing environmental impacts, and aligning with the principles of the bioeconomy. As cities grow and become increasingly dependent on complex global networks for food, they are vulnerable to disruptions caused by climate change, pandemics, geopolitical instability, and economic shocks. Building resilience into food supply chains involves strengthening local production, diversifying sources, reducing waste, and integrating circular bioeconomic practices. These strategies not only secure reliable access to food but also create opportunities for innovation and sustainability in urban economies.

One of the key elements of resilience is localization of food systems. While cities will always rely to some extent on global trade, expanding local and regional production reduces vulnerability to external disruptions. Urban agriculture, vertical farming, aquaponics, and peri-urban farming create decentralized food production systems that supplement imports. By producing food closer to consumers, these systems reduce transport emissions, shorten supply chains, and ensure fresher produce. Localization also strengthens the connection between consumers and producers, fostering trust and supporting local economies.

Diversification is another critical dimension. Resilient food supply chains avoid overdependence on a narrow range of crops, suppliers, or trade routes. Encouraging dietary diversity and supporting a variety of bio-based food products reduces risk and improves adaptability. For example, promoting alternative proteins such as legumes, insects, or lab-grown meat reduces pressure on conventional livestock systems that are resource-intensive and vulnerable to disease outbreaks. Similarly, diversifying sourcing strategies ensures that disruptions in one region do not destabilize entire urban food networks.

Waste reduction is central to resilience and the bioeconomy. A significant proportion of food produced globally is lost or wasted, with urban areas contributing heavily to the problem. Efficient logistics, cold-chain infrastructure, and digital tools for tracking supply flows can reduce spoilage and inefficiency. Food recovery programs that redistribute surplus food to those in need improve social equity while lowering waste. Inedible fractions can be valorized into compost, bioenergy, or animal feed, reintegrating them into circular resource loops. This approach maximizes the utility of food resources while reducing environmental burdens.

Technology enhances the resilience of urban food supply chains by improving transparency and efficiency. Digital platforms connect consumers to local producers, reducing reliance on intermediaries and enabling just-in-time delivery. Blockchain systems ensure traceability, giving consumers confidence in the sustainability and safety of their food. Artificial intelligence and predictive analytics optimize supply chain management, anticipating disruptions and adjusting sourcing or distribution accordingly. These tools increase responsiveness and adaptability, key qualities of resilient systems.

Governance and policy frameworks are equally important. Municipalities can support resilience by creating enabling environments for urban farming, investing in food logistics infrastructure, and enacting regulations that encourage sustainable sourcing and waste reduction. Public procurement policies that prioritize local and bio-based products stimulate demand and provide stable markets for producers. Collaborative governance involving governments, businesses, civil society, and communities ensures that resilience strategies are inclusive and reflect diverse needs.

Resilient urban food supply chains are not only about ensuring consistent food supply; they represent a systemic rethinking of how cities interact with biological resources. By prioritizing localization, diversification, waste reduction, and circularity, cities can build food systems that are robust, adaptive, and aligned with the goals of the urban bioeconomy. These supply chains strengthen sustainability, support innovation, and ensure that urban populations are nourished in ways that respect ecological and social boundaries.

Chapter 6: Energy and Mobility Transitions

Energy and mobility transitions are central to achieving the goals of the urban bioeconomy, reshaping how cities power their infrastructure and move people and goods. Conventional systems, heavily dependent on fossil fuels, are responsible for significant greenhouse gas emissions, air pollution, and resource inefficiencies. By integrating renewable energy, bioenergy, electrification, and sustainable transport, cities can decarbonize their economies while enhancing resilience and quality of life. This chapter explores how energy and mobility systems can evolve together, highlighting the synergies between bio-based solutions, technological innovation, and policy frameworks that support sustainable and inclusive urban transformation.

Bioenergy and Renewable Integration in Cities

Bioenergy and renewable integration are key pillars of the urban bioeconomy, enabling cities to transition from fossil-based energy systems to sustainable, resilient, and low-carbon models. With rising energy demands and the challenges of climate change, urban areas require solutions that not only decarbonize their energy supply but also embed circularity by using biological resources efficiently. Bioenergy—derived from organic waste, biomass, and other renewable feedstocks—plays a crucial role in complementing other renewable sources such as solar and wind, creating diversified and reliable energy systems.

A major advantage of bioenergy in urban contexts is its ability to convert waste streams into usable energy. Organic waste from households, food industries, and wastewater treatment plants can be processed through anaerobic digestion or gasification to produce biogas, which can generate electricity, provide heating, or serve as a renewable substitute for natural gas. This approach not only reduces landfill use and methane emissions but also turns a costly urban problem into a valuable resource. By integrating bioenergy facilities into city infrastructure, waste management, energy production, and nutrient recovery can be linked into closed-loop systems.

Bioenergy also enhances the integration of renewables by providing stability to urban energy grids. Solar and wind power are variable, depending on weather conditions and time of day, while bioenergy can supply constant, dispatchable power. Cities that combine intermittent renewables with bioenergy create balanced systems capable of meeting demand reliably. For example, biogas from organic waste can be stored and released when solar or wind output is low, ensuring continuity of supply. This complementarity strengthens resilience and reduces dependence on fossil fuel backup systems.

District heating and cooling systems provide another application of bioenergy in cities. Heat generated from biomass or waste-to-energy plants can be distributed through networks to supply residential, commercial, and industrial buildings. Coupling these systems with combined heat and power plants increases efficiency by producing electricity and heat simultaneously. When integrated with renewable sources such as geothermal or solar thermal energy, district systems offer a scalable pathway to decarbonize urban heating and cooling, which represent significant shares of energy consumption in cities.

Policy frameworks and governance are vital for integrating bioenergy with renewables in urban areas. Municipalities can provide incentives for bioenergy projects, support feed-in tariffs for biogas and biomass electricity, and set renewable energy targets that encourage innovation. Public-private partnerships are particularly effective, combining municipal oversight with private-sector investment and expertise. Aligning bioenergy strategies with broader urban sustainability plans ensures that energy transitions are integrated with waste management, transportation, and housing policies.

Social and economic benefits further reinforce the value of bioenergy in cities. Local bioenergy projects create jobs in waste collection, processing, and plant operation, while reducing dependence on imported fuels enhances energy security. Communities benefit from improved air quality, cleaner environments, and more reliable energy supplies. Public engagement in waste separation and renewable adoption also fosters a culture of sustainability, embedding bioeconomic principles into daily urban life.

Bioenergy and renewable integration in cities therefore exemplify how urban systems can transition to circular, regenerative models. By linking waste management with energy production, and by complementing variable renewable sources, bioenergy supports the creation of reliable, low-carbon energy systems. This integration strengthens resilience, reduces emissions, and positions cities as leaders in sustainable energy innovation.

Biofuels for Sustainable Transport

Biofuels play a significant role in advancing sustainable transport within cities, providing renewable alternatives to fossil-based fuels while contributing to the broader goals of the urban bioeconomy. Transport remains one of the largest sources of greenhouse gas emissions in urban areas, driven by reliance on petroleum-based fuels. Biofuels derived from renewable biological resources such as crops, algae, waste oils, and organic residues offer a pathway to decarbonize mobility systems, reduce air pollution, and integrate circularity into urban energy flows.

First-generation biofuels, produced from food crops like corn and sugarcane, laid the foundation for renewable transport fuels. However, their competition with food production raised concerns about land use and food security. More advanced second- and third-generation biofuels, derived from non-food biomass such as agricultural residues, lignocellulosic materials, and algae, address these issues by tapping into resources that would otherwise be discarded. These fuels can be used in existing vehicles and infrastructure, making them particularly suitable for urban fleets where electrification may not yet be fully feasible.

One of the main applications of biofuels in cities is in public transportation systems. Buses, municipal fleets, and even taxis can be powered by biodiesel or bioethanol, reducing emissions and dependence on imported fossil fuels. Waste-to-biofuel initiatives in urban areas highlight the circularity of this approach: used cooking oil from restaurants or organic waste from households can be converted into biodiesel, creating a local and renewable energy source. This integration reduces waste disposal challenges while contributing to sustainable mobility.

Aviation and freight transport, sectors that are difficult to electrify, also benefit from biofuels. Sustainable aviation fuels derived from waste oils or algae are increasingly recognized as essential for reducing emissions from air travel. Similarly, biofuels provide an interim solution for heavy trucks and shipping while electrification and hydrogen technologies continue to mature. By incorporating biofuels into these hard-to-abate sectors, cities and regions can advance toward decarbonization targets while maintaining mobility and economic activity.

Biofuels also play a complementary role alongside other renewable energy solutions. While electrification is expanding rapidly, it faces challenges related to infrastructure, battery technology, and resource availability. Biofuels offer a flexible option that can be integrated into existing systems and combined with electricity to create hybrid approaches. For example, biofuel-powered generators can support electric vehicle charging stations, ensuring reliability during peak demand or when renewable electricity supply is variable. This flexibility strengthens urban energy resilience.

Policy frameworks are essential to promote the use of biofuels in sustainable transport. Governments can incentivize adoption through subsidies, blending mandates, tax benefits, and public procurement requirements. Standards and certification schemes ensure that biofuels meet sustainability criteria, addressing concerns about deforestation, biodiversity loss, and indirect land-use change. Municipal initiatives, such as mandating biofuels for public transport fleets, create stable demand and encourage investment in local biofuel production facilities.

Social and economic benefits further support biofuels in cities. Local production generates jobs in collection, processing, and distribution, while reducing reliance on imported fossil fuels enhances energy security. Improved air quality from lower particulate and sulfur emissions benefits urban populations, particularly vulnerable groups. Public engagement through waste-to-fuel programs also fosters community involvement in circular bioeconomic practices.

Biofuels for sustainable transport therefore represent a practical and scalable solution within the urban bioeconomy. By converting biological resources and waste streams into renewable fuels, cities can reduce emissions, improve air quality, and diversify their energy systems. They provide an essential bridge toward long-term decarbonization, complementing electrification and other renewable innovations in the transition to sustainable mobility.

Electrification and Bio-Based Mobility Synergies

Electrification and bio-based mobility are often viewed as parallel strategies for decarbonizing transport, but in reality, they complement each other in creating resilient, low-carbon urban mobility systems. Electrification reduces direct emissions from vehicles and improves air quality, while bio-based mobility provides renewable alternatives for sectors or contexts where electrification alone is insufficient. Together, they create synergies that enhance flexibility, circularity, and resilience in urban transport systems, making them central to the urban bioeconomy.

Electrification is rapidly transforming urban mobility through the adoption of electric cars, buses, trams, and bikes. Its benefits include lower operational emissions, reduced noise pollution, and integration with renewable electricity grids. However, electrification faces challenges such as the carbon footprint of battery production, limited raw material availability, and the need for extensive charging infrastructure. Bio-based mobility solutions, particularly advanced biofuels, address these gaps by offering renewable liquid fuels that can be used in existing engines and infrastructure. This is particularly important for heavy-duty vehicles, aviation, and freight transport, which are harder to electrify due to energy density and range requirements.

The synergies between electrification and bio-based mobility become evident when considering system integration. For example, biofuels and biogas can provide backup energy for electric vehicle charging networks, ensuring reliability when renewable electricity supply fluctuates. Similarly, electrified vehicles can operate in tandem with biofuel-powered logistics fleets, diversifying energy sources and reducing vulnerability to supply disruptions. This combination creates resilient urban transport systems capable of adapting to different conditions while minimizing reliance on fossil fuels.

Resource efficiency is another area of synergy. Organic waste streams from cities can be converted into biogas or biodiesel to fuel municipal buses or garbage trucks, while the electricity grid increasingly relies on solar, wind, and other renewables. Together, these systems embody circularity by ensuring that urban waste becomes a resource for mobility. At the same time, electrification reduces overall energy demand by improving efficiency, making it easier for bio-based fuels to target specific sectors where they provide the most impact.

Governance and policy frameworks are critical for fostering these synergies. Integrated urban mobility plans can set targets for both electrification and biofuel use, ensuring that the two strategies complement rather than compete. Incentives for electric vehicle adoption can be paired with mandates for renewable fuel blends, while public procurement policies can prioritize both electric and biofuel-powered fleets. Partnerships between energy providers, waste managers, and transport authorities enable coordinated planning that maximizes the potential of both technologies.

Social and economic benefits also emerge from this integration. Electrification reduces local air pollution, improving health outcomes in densely populated areas, while bio-based fuels create jobs in waste collection, processing, and biofuel production. Both strategies enhance energy security by reducing dependence on imported fossil fuels and diversifying urban energy portfolios. Public engagement in initiatives such as community biogas projects or shared electric mobility services further strengthens participation in the bioeconomy.

Electrification and bio-based mobility synergies demonstrate that urban transport transitions do not require a single solution but rather a portfolio of complementary strategies. By combining the efficiency of electric systems with the flexibility of bio-based fuels, cities can create integrated, circular, and resilient mobility networks that align with the goals of the urban bioeconomy.

Urban Energy Efficiency and Bio-Based Solutions

Energy efficiency is a cornerstone of sustainable urban development, reducing resource consumption, lowering emissions, and minimizing costs for households, businesses, and municipalities. When combined with bio-based solutions, energy efficiency contributes directly to the goals of the urban bioeconomy by embedding circularity and renewable resource use into energy systems. This integration enables cities to meet rising energy demands while decarbonizing infrastructure and fostering innovation.

At its core, urban energy efficiency involves designing systems and practices that reduce the amount of energy required to provide essential services. Buildings, transportation, and industrial activities consume the majority of urban energy, and improving their efficiency is critical to reducing emissions. Strategies include retrofitting buildings with insulation and efficient lighting, optimizing heating and cooling systems, and incorporating smart grids that balance supply and demand. These measures not only reduce energy intensity but also create opportunities for incorporating bio-based resources into urban systems.

Bio-based solutions strengthen energy efficiency by providing renewable alternatives that integrate seamlessly with efficient technologies. For example, bio-based insulation materials such as hemp, cellulose, or sheep wool improve building performance while reducing reliance on energy-intensive synthetic products. Green roofs and walls, constructed with vegetation, add thermal efficiency by regulating building temperatures naturally, lowering the need for air conditioning and heating. These approaches demonstrate how bio-based materials and natural processes can reduce urban energy demand while contributing to biodiversity and climate resilience.

Energy recovery from organic waste is another area where bio-based solutions enhance efficiency. Urban food waste, wastewater sludge, and other organic materials can be converted into biogas through anaerobic digestion, generating renewable electricity and heat. This process not only recycles waste but also reduces reliance on fossil fuels for energy production. Coupling waste-to-energy systems with efficient district heating and cooling networks ensures that energy is used effectively and sustainably. These synergies exemplify the principles of urban metabolism, where waste flows are reimagined as valuable energy sources.

Transport systems also benefit from combining efficiency measures with bio-based solutions. While electrification is expanding rapidly, biofuels derived from urban organic residues or waste oils can provide renewable energy for public buses, municipal fleets, and freight vehicles that are harder to electrify. Improving logistics efficiency through digital platforms, route optimization, and shared mobility reduces fuel demand, while biofuels supply a renewable option for the remaining needs. Together, these strategies lower emissions, cut costs, and strengthen energy resilience in cities.

Governance and policy support are essential to accelerate the integration of energy efficiency and bio-based solutions. Building codes that require renewable insulation materials, incentives for green infrastructure, and procurement policies that favor bio-based products all create stable demand. Municipal energy strategies can set targets for efficiency improvements alongside renewable integration, ensuring coherent progress. Collaboration among public agencies, businesses, and communities ensures that policies reflect diverse needs while fostering innovation.

Energy efficiency combined with bio-based solutions demonstrates how urban areas can reduce energy demand, integrate renewable resources, and create resilient systems. This dual strategy transforms energy management from a purely technical challenge into a holistic approach that aligns environmental, social, and economic objectives. By embedding efficiency and bio-based innovation into urban planning, cities can lead the way toward sustainable and regenerative energy futures.

Resilient and Low-Carbon Urban Transport Systems

Resilient and low-carbon urban transport systems are central to the transition toward sustainable cities and the realization of the urban bioeconomy. Transport is a major source of greenhouse gas emissions, air pollution, and resource consumption, while also being essential for economic activity and social connectivity. Reimagining urban mobility requires reducing dependence on fossil fuels, enhancing efficiency, and ensuring that systems can withstand shocks from climate change, economic disruptions, and demographic shifts. By integrating low-carbon technologies with resilient design, cities can create transport systems that are sustainable, equitable, and future-ready.

One of the key strategies for low-carbon transport is diversification of mobility options. Electrification of vehicles, including buses, trams, and private cars, reduces emissions and air pollution, while biofuels derived from waste and renewable resources provide an alternative for sectors less suited to electrification, such as freight and aviation. Active mobility options like walking and cycling further reduce energy demand while contributing to public health. A resilient transport system ensures that these modes are interconnected, offering flexibility and redundancy that reduce vulnerability to disruptions.

Urban design also plays a crucial role in shaping transport systems. Compact, mixed-use development reduces travel distances and supports low-carbon modes such as walking, cycling, and public transit. Transit-oriented development clusters housing, jobs, and services around public transport hubs, creating efficient networks that minimize reliance on private vehicles. Green infrastructure, such as shaded bike lanes and permeable pavements, enhances climate resilience by mitigating heat stress and managing stormwater. By embedding transport planning within urban design, cities ensure that mobility systems are integrated with ecological and social priorities.

Technology strengthens both resilience and decarbonization in urban transport. Smart traffic management systems optimize flows, reducing congestion and emissions. Digital platforms support shared mobility services, reducing the number of vehicles needed while improving accessibility. Data analytics and predictive modeling allow cities to anticipate demand and respond to disruptions quickly, enhancing adaptability. When paired with renewable energy integration, these innovations ensure that low-carbon transport systems are not only efficient but also responsive to dynamic urban conditions.

Governance and policy frameworks are critical enablers of resilient, low-carbon transport. Municipal authorities can establish emissions reduction targets, implement congestion pricing, and provide subsidies for low-carbon vehicles and infrastructure. Public procurement policies that prioritize electric or biofuel-powered fleets demonstrate leadership and create stable demand. Partnerships between governments, businesses, and communities ensure that transport systems reflect diverse needs while distributing benefits equitably. Resilience planning, including scenario analysis and emergency preparedness, ensures that transport systems can withstand shocks from climate extremes or energy supply disruptions.

Social inclusion is a vital dimension of resilient transport systems. Low-carbon mobility must be affordable and accessible to all residents, reducing inequalities in access to jobs, education, and services. Investments in reliable public transit, safe pedestrian infrastructure, and affordable shared mobility options ensure that sustainability benefits are shared widely. Community participation in planning processes also strengthens social resilience, aligning transport solutions with local needs and priorities.

Resilient and low-carbon urban transport systems therefore embody the principles of the urban bioeconomy: circularity, renewable resource use, and social inclusivity. By diversifying mobility options, integrating with urban design, leveraging technology, and ensuring equitable access, cities can build transport systems that are both sustainable and adaptable. These systems not only reduce emissions but also create healthier, more resilient, and more livable urban environments.

Chapter 7: Biotechnology and Innovation

Biotechnology is a cornerstone of the urban bioeconomy, offering transformative tools for creating sustainable, circular, and regenerative systems in cities. By harnessing biological processes and engineering capabilities, biotechnology enables the development of renewable materials, bio-based energy, innovative healthcare solutions, and advanced waste-to-resource pathways. Innovation in this field not only supports environmental goals but also drives economic competitiveness and resilience, opening new industries and employment opportunities. This chapter explores the diverse applications of biotechnology in urban contexts, highlighting how innovation accelerates the adoption of bio-based solutions and integrates them into the fabric of sustainable city development.

Biotechnology in Urban Applications

Biotechnology is increasingly shaping urban systems by offering innovative solutions that integrate biological processes with city infrastructure, industries, and services. As part of the urban bioeconomy, biotechnology enables cities to become more sustainable, resilient, and efficient by addressing challenges such as waste management, energy generation, healthcare, and environmental quality. The versatility of biotechnology allows it to operate at multiple scales—from molecular innovations to city-wide systems—making it a transformative force in urban development.

One major application of biotechnology in cities is waste management and resource recovery. Microbial and enzymatic processes are used to break down organic waste into biogas, fertilizers, and bio-based chemicals. Advances in synthetic biology are enabling engineered microbes to recover valuable compounds such as phosphorus or to convert waste streams into biofuels. These approaches close nutrient and energy loops, reducing landfill use and aligning urban metabolism with circular economy principles. Wastewater treatment plants are increasingly being redesigned as bio-based resource hubs, recovering water, energy, and nutrients simultaneously.

Energy systems also benefit from biotechnology. Bioenergy derived from algae, microbial fuel cells, and anaerobic digestion provides renewable power while reducing reliance on fossil fuels. Cities with dense populations generate abundant organic waste and wastewater, both of which serve as feedstocks for bioenergy. In addition, biotechnological innovations are expanding the potential of biohydrogen and advanced biofuels, which can complement electrification and support sectors like freight and aviation that are harder to decarbonize. By embedding biotechnology into energy systems, cities can create decentralized, renewable power sources that strengthen resilience.

Healthcare and public health are other domains where biotechnology has profound impacts in urban settings. Rapid diagnostic tools, genetic sequencing, and bio-based pharmaceuticals enhance the ability of cities to respond to public health crises. Biotechnology also contributes to personalized medicine and disease monitoring, which are increasingly important in densely populated areas. On a broader scale, biotechnological tools are used for monitoring urban air and water quality, employing biosensors and engineered organisms to detect pollutants and pathogens in real time. This integration supports healthier urban environments and better-informed decision-making.

Construction and materials science also draw on biotechnology to reduce environmental impacts. Bio-based materials such as mycelium composites, bioplastics, and bio-concrete are being developed as alternatives to conventional, carbon-intensive materials. These innovations not only lower emissions but also offer new functionalities such as biodegradability or self-healing properties. Incorporating biotechnology into urban construction supports circular design and creates opportunities for regenerative buildings that interact positively with ecosystems.

Governance and policy frameworks play a vital role in mainstreaming biotechnology in urban applications. Standards and regulations ensure safety, quality, and social acceptance of bio-based innovations. Public-private partnerships support research, development, and deployment of technologies at scale, while citizen engagement builds trust and fosters participation in bio-based initiatives such as community composting or urban agriculture powered by biotechnology. Education and workforce training also ensure that the benefits of biotechnology are widely shared and that new industries have the skilled labor they require.

Biotechnology in urban applications demonstrates how biology, technology, and governance can be combined to address complex challenges in cities. From waste valorization and renewable energy to healthcare and materials innovation, biotechnology contributes to creating urban environments that are efficient, resilient, and regenerative. Its integration into urban systems reflects the broader vision of the bioeconomy, where natural processes and human innovation work together to build sustainable futures.

Synthetic Biology and Resource Efficiency

Synthetic biology is an emerging field that combines principles of engineering, biology, and digital design to create or reprogram biological systems for new functions. Within the context of the urban bioeconomy, synthetic biology has enormous potential to enhance resource efficiency by enabling the development of renewable materials, optimizing waste-to-resource processes, and reducing dependence on fossil-based inputs. By designing organisms and biological processes with specific capabilities, synthetic biology allows cities to address resource constraints in innovative and sustainable ways.

One of the most promising contributions of synthetic biology is the development of bio-based materials that replace energy- and resource-intensive conventional products. Engineered microbes and yeast strains can be programmed to produce bioplastics, textiles, and chemicals from renewable biomass. For example, synthetic biology enables the production of polylactic acid and other biodegradable polymers, which reduce reliance on petrochemicals and minimize plastic pollution in cities. These materials not only contribute to circular urban economies but also offer improved performance characteristics such as biodegradability or reduced toxicity, enhancing environmental and public health outcomes.

Synthetic biology also improves efficiency in waste valorization processes. Urban organic waste, wastewater, and agricultural residues can be converted into valuable products through engineered microbial systems. Microorganisms can be designed to digest complex waste materials more effectively, yielding higher outputs of biogas, biofuels, or high-value compounds such as enzymes and vitamins. By closing loops between waste generation and resource recovery, synthetic biology reduces the amount of waste destined for landfills while increasing the productivity of urban resource systems.

In food systems, synthetic biology enhances resource efficiency by enabling sustainable alternatives to traditional agriculture and livestock production. Engineered microbes can produce proteins, fats, and other food components with far less land, water, and energy than conventional farming. Precision fermentation allows for the creation of dairy or meat substitutes that replicate the nutritional and sensory qualities of animal products without the associated environmental footprint. For cities, where demand for food is high and space is limited, these innovations contribute to resilient and resource-efficient food supply chains.

Energy systems also benefit from synthetic biology. Engineered algae and bacteria can be optimized to produce biofuels or hydrogen more efficiently, using waste carbon dioxide or organic matter as feedstock. These technologies not only provide renewable energy sources but also help mitigate urban emissions by capturing and repurposing greenhouse gases. Integrating synthetic biology with urban energy systems thus strengthens both circularity and decarbonization efforts.

Governance and ethical considerations are crucial for advancing synthetic biology in urban applications. Ensuring biosafety, transparency, and public trust is essential to avoid risks and to promote acceptance of bio-based innovations. Standards and certification schemes can guarantee that products meet safety and sustainability criteria. Collaboration between governments, research institutions, and private firms fosters responsible innovation while ensuring that benefits are equitably distributed.

Synthetic biology represents a transformative pathway for improving resource efficiency in cities. By enabling the design of biological systems that produce renewable materials, valorize waste, and optimize energy and food systems, it advances the principles of the bioeconomy. When integrated responsibly, synthetic biology can help urban areas reduce environmental impacts, conserve resources, and build resilient and sustainable futures.

Urban Health and Bio-Based Medical Innovations

Urban health is a growing priority as cities expand and face complex challenges such as pollution, high population density, and unequal access to healthcare. The bioeconomy offers opportunities to improve urban health outcomes through bio-based medical innovations that harness biological processes and renewable resources to deliver sustainable, effective, and inclusive solutions. These innovations not only address immediate medical needs but also align healthcare systems with broader goals of circularity, resilience, and sustainability.

One of the most significant contributions of the bioeconomy to urban health is the development of bio-based pharmaceuticals and therapeutics. Advances in biotechnology and synthetic biology enable the production of vaccines, antibiotics, and therapeutic proteins using engineered microbes, algae, or plants as biological factories. These processes reduce reliance on fossil-derived chemicals and energy-intensive manufacturing while making medicines more scalable and adaptable. For cities, where the demand for healthcare is high, bio-based pharmaceuticals provide a sustainable foundation for addressing both routine care and emergency responses such as pandemics.

Diagnostics and monitoring also benefit from bio-based innovations. Biosensors, which use biological components to detect pathogens, toxins, or pollutants, provide rapid and precise diagnostic tools. In urban settings, biosensors can be deployed in hospitals, clinics, and even public spaces to monitor health risks in real time. Wastewater epidemiology, which relies on biotechnology to analyze viral and bacterial markers in sewage, has proven valuable for tracking infectious disease outbreaks in cities. These approaches enable proactive public health strategies, reducing risks before they escalate into crises.

Bio-based medical technologies also contribute to regenerative medicine and advanced treatments. Tissue engineering, which uses biodegradable scaffolds and stem cells, allows for the repair or replacement of damaged organs and tissues. Bioprinting technologies are advancing the development of patient-specific implants and grafts, offering urban populations access to cutting-edge healthcare solutions. By reducing reliance on synthetic or non-renewable materials, these innovations improve sustainability while delivering personalized care.

Environmental health is another dimension where bio-based innovations support urban well-being. Air and water quality directly affect public health, and biotechnology provides tools to monitor and mitigate pollution. Engineered microorganisms can be deployed to clean contaminated water or soils, while bio-based air filters can capture pollutants more effectively than conventional systems. These approaches integrate healthcare with environmental management, recognizing the interdependence of human health and ecological systems in cities.

Governance, equity, and access are critical considerations in deploying bio-based medical innovations in urban areas. Municipal health policies can support the adoption of sustainable healthcare practices, from incentivizing bio-based procurement to funding research in local universities and hospitals. Ensuring equitable access to these innovations is essential, as disparities in urban healthcare can exacerbate social inequality. Community engagement, transparency, and public education build trust in bio-based approaches, ensuring that their benefits are widely shared across urban populations.

Bio-based medical innovations demonstrate how health systems can be aligned with the principles of the bioeconomy. By reducing environmental impacts, enhancing resilience, and creating inclusive access to care, these innovations strengthen the capacity of cities to address both current and future health challenges. They highlight the potential for biotechnology, regenerative practices, and bio-based solutions to create urban healthcare systems that are sustainable, adaptable, and responsive to the needs of growing populations.

Innovations in Bio-Based Plastics and Alternatives

Plastics are integral to modern urban life, yet their widespread use and persistence in the environment have created significant ecological and social challenges. Conventional plastics, derived from fossil fuels, contribute heavily to carbon emissions, waste accumulation, and pollution in oceans and cities. Innovations in bio-based plastics and alternatives are reshaping this landscape, offering renewable, biodegradable, and recyclable options that align with the principles of the bioeconomy. These materials provide cities with sustainable solutions for packaging, construction, consumer goods, and beyond, while helping to close resource loops and reduce environmental pressures.

Bio-based plastics are typically produced from renewable feedstocks such as corn starch, sugarcane, cellulose, or even algae. Polylactic acid (PLA) and polyhydroxyalkanoates (PHA) are among the most prominent examples. PLA is widely used for packaging, disposable cutlery, and textiles, offering biodegradability under industrial composting conditions. PHA, produced by bacterial fermentation of organic materials, is fully biodegradable and has properties comparable to conventional plastics, making it suitable for medical, agricultural, and packaging applications. These innovations reduce dependence on fossil resources while enabling new value chains from urban organic waste streams.

Advanced research is expanding the possibilities for bio-based plastics. Scientists are engineering microbes to produce polymers with tailored properties, enhancing strength, flexibility, or heat resistance. Algae-derived plastics offer additional promise, as algae can grow rapidly with minimal inputs, including wastewater or carbon dioxide, while simultaneously capturing emissions. These breakthroughs highlight the role of biotechnology and synthetic biology in creating next-generation materials that not only substitute fossil-based plastics but also integrate into circular urban systems.

Alternatives to plastics go beyond direct substitutes and include innovative materials that provide similar functionality without the environmental costs. Edible packaging made from seaweed, starch, or other bio-based materials eliminates waste altogether. Biodegradable films for food wrapping, developed from proteins or polysaccharides, offer sustainable options for urban food systems. Mycelium-based materials, created from fungal growth, can replace polystyrene in packaging or be molded into durable products for construction and design. These alternatives expand the scope of solutions, ensuring that urban economies can reduce reliance on single-use plastics while fostering innovation in materials science.

Urban applications of bio-based plastics and alternatives are growing rapidly. Cities, as major consumers of packaged goods, are well positioned to drive adoption through procurement policies, waste management systems, and consumer awareness campaigns. Municipal regulations banning single-use plastics often create market space for bio-based substitutes, while investment in composting and recycling infrastructure ensures that these materials are properly managed at the end of their life. By linking production, consumption, and disposal within circular frameworks, cities can embed bio-based plastics into sustainable urban metabolism.

Policy support, governance, and market development are essential for scaling innovations in bio-based plastics. Standards and certifications that verify biodegradability and sustainability ensure consumer trust and prevent greenwashing. Incentives for research, manufacturing, and infrastructure investment accelerate adoption, while public education campaigns encourage behavioral change. Collaboration across industries, governments, and communities strengthens innovation ecosystems, making bio-based plastics a practical and scalable solution for cities.

Innovations in bio-based plastics and alternatives demonstrate the potential of the bioeconomy to transform one of the most persistent urban challenges. By replacing fossil-based products with renewable, biodegradable, and functional substitutes, cities can reduce pollution, lower emissions, and create new economic opportunities. These materials illustrate how circular and regenerative principles can be applied to everyday products, reshaping urban consumption and production in line with sustainable futures.

Role of Research and Development Ecosystems

Research and development (R&D) ecosystems are fundamental to advancing the urban bioeconomy, providing the knowledge, innovation, and collaboration required to create sustainable and circular solutions. In rapidly urbanizing environments, where challenges such as resource scarcity, pollution, and climate change are most acute, R&D ecosystems function as incubators for new technologies, materials, and practices. By linking universities, research institutes, private companies, startups, and government agencies, they accelerate the development and deployment of bio-based innovations that align with the needs of cities.

At the heart of R&D ecosystems is the generation of new knowledge and technologies. Universities and research centers conduct basic and applied research in areas such as biotechnology, synthetic biology, renewable energy, and bio-based materials. These institutions push the boundaries of science, discovering new ways to valorize organic waste, design biodegradable products, or enhance energy efficiency. Applied research ensures that these discoveries move beyond the laboratory to address real-world challenges in urban contexts, such as waste management, air quality, or food security.

Collaboration across sectors is a defining characteristic of effective R&D ecosystems. No single actor can advance the bioeconomy alone, as it spans multiple domains—agriculture, energy, healthcare, construction, and manufacturing. Public-private partnerships provide platforms where governments offer funding and regulatory support, businesses contribute expertise and market access, and research institutions supply innovation and technical knowledge. These collaborations ensure that R&D efforts are aligned with market needs while also contributing to public goods such as environmental protection and social equity.

Innovation hubs, incubators, and living labs serve as critical nodes within R&D ecosystems. They provide environments where new technologies can be tested, refined, and demonstrated under real-world urban conditions. Living labs, for example, allow residents, businesses, and researchers to co-create solutions such as decentralized bioenergy systems, vertical farms, or biorefineries. By integrating experimentation with everyday urban life, these spaces accelerate adoption and build trust in bio-based innovations.

Financing and investment are also integral to R&D ecosystems. Governments and international organizations often provide grants and subsidies to de-risk early-stage research and innovation. Venture capital and impact investors then help scale promising technologies into viable businesses. In urban settings, local authorities can attract investment by supporting R&D clusters, providing infrastructure, and offering favorable regulatory environments. These financial mechanisms ensure that the innovation pipeline flows from discovery to commercialization, making bioeconomic solutions accessible and scalable.

Capacity building is another critical role of R&D ecosystems. By training students, entrepreneurs, and workers in bioeconomy-related fields, universities and institutions prepare a skilled workforce for emerging industries. Education programs that emphasize interdisciplinary skills—combining biology, engineering, economics, and policy—equip individuals to navigate the complex challenges of the urban bioeconomy. Public engagement and science communication further strengthen these ecosystems, ensuring that citizens understand and support the role of bio-based innovations in their communities.

The role of R&D ecosystems in advancing the bioeconomy is therefore multifaceted. They generate knowledge, foster collaboration, provide testing grounds, mobilize investment, and build human capacity. By embedding innovation into urban systems, R&D ecosystems ensure that bio-based solutions are not only developed but also implemented and scaled. Their contributions enable cities to transition toward regenerative, low-carbon, and resilient futures, positioning research and innovation at the core of sustainable urban transformation.

Chapter 8: Financing the Urban Bioeconomy

Financing is one of the most decisive factors in enabling the transition toward an urban bioeconomy. While technological innovations, governance structures, and policy frameworks provide the vision and tools, it is financing mechanisms that determine whether projects can move from concept to implementation at scale. Bioeconomic initiatives often require substantial upfront investment in infrastructure, research, and capacity building, while their long-term benefits are spread across environmental, social, and economic dimensions. This chapter examines the diverse financing approaches—from public funds and private capital to blended finance and innovative instruments—that underpin the growth of urban bio-based systems.

Green Bonds and Sustainable Finance Instruments

Green bonds and other sustainable finance instruments are powerful enablers of the urban bioeconomy, channeling capital toward projects that advance environmental and social goals. As cities face growing demands for infrastructure, energy, and services while grappling with climate change and resource scarcity, financing mechanisms that prioritize sustainability are essential. Green bonds, along with related instruments such as sustainability-linked loans, social bonds, and blended finance vehicles, provide the means to mobilize investment for bio-based solutions, circular systems, and resilient urban development.

Green bonds are debt instruments specifically earmarked to fund projects with environmental benefits. In urban contexts, these projects often include renewable energy facilities, energy-efficient buildings, green infrastructure, waste valorization plants, and sustainable transport systems. By labeling bonds as "green," issuers signal their commitment to sustainability, attracting investors who seek both financial returns and positive environmental impacts. Transparency and reporting requirements ensure accountability, making green bonds a trusted mechanism for financing bioeconomic initiatives. For cities, issuing green bonds allows them to access capital markets to fund large-scale projects that align with long-term sustainability goals.

Beyond green bonds, other sustainable finance instruments are gaining traction. Sustainability-linked loans tie borrowing costs to the achievement of specific environmental or social targets, incentivizing organizations to improve performance. Social bonds finance projects that deliver social benefits such as affordable housing or healthcare, often linked to broader sustainability agendas. Blended finance mechanisms combine public and private capital to de-risk investments in innovative or early-stage bioeconomic technologies, ensuring that transformative projects receive the funding needed to scale. Together, these instruments create a diverse toolkit for financing sustainable urban development.

One of the strengths of sustainable finance instruments is their ability to align investor interests with bioeconomic outcomes. Institutional investors, including pension funds and insurance companies, are increasingly incorporating environmental, social, and governance (ESG) criteria into their portfolios. By providing well-structured and transparent instruments, cities and businesses can tap into this growing pool of capital. This alignment not only mobilizes resources for bio-based projects but also signals a broader cultural shift in finance toward recognizing the value of sustainability and resilience.

The impact of green bonds and sustainable finance instruments extends beyond funding. They also create market signals that shape priorities for both public and private actors. By issuing green bonds for bio-based infrastructure, cities set benchmarks that encourage further innovation and investment in sustainable technologies. Standards and taxonomies developed at the international level ensure that financed projects deliver measurable environmental benefits, reducing the risk of "greenwashing." These frameworks enhance trust, attract investors, and create consistency across markets.

Challenges remain, including the need to expand access for smaller municipalities and developing cities that may lack creditworthiness or capacity to issue bonds. Technical assistance, capacity building, and partnerships with development banks can help overcome these barriers. Scaling sustainable finance also requires continuous improvement in transparency, reporting, and impact measurement to ensure credibility.

Green bonds and sustainable finance instruments are therefore more than tools for raising capital—they are catalysts for systemic change. By directing resources toward circular, bio-based, and resilient projects, they empower cities to build infrastructures and economies that thrive within ecological boundaries. Their role in the urban bioeconomy highlights the importance of aligning financial flows with sustainability, ensuring that investment supports not only economic returns but also environmental and social well-being.

Impact Investment and Bioeconomic Enterprises

Impact investment has become a driving force in financing sustainable urban transformation, directing capital toward businesses and initiatives that generate measurable social and environmental benefits alongside financial returns. In the context of the urban bioeconomy, impact investors play a pivotal role in supporting bioeconomic enterprises that apply biological resources and circular principles to address urban challenges such as waste, energy, food, and health. By aligning profit with purpose, impact investment fosters innovation, accelerates the adoption of bio-based solutions, and builds resilient, low-carbon cities.

Bioeconomic enterprises operate across a wide range of sectors, offering products and services that contribute to sustainability while creating economic opportunities. Startups are developing biodegradable packaging from algae, fungi, or agricultural residues to replace plastics in urban markets. Companies are building biorefineries that convert organic waste into energy, fertilizers, and bio-based chemicals, reducing reliance on fossil-based industries.

Urban agriculture enterprises use hydroponics, aquaponics, and vertical farming to produce fresh food locally, lowering transport emissions and strengthening food security. In healthcare, bio-based enterprises develop biopharmaceuticals, diagnostics, and regenerative treatments, ensuring that health systems in cities evolve sustainably.

Impact investment provides these enterprises with the capital needed to scale. Traditional financing often views bioeconomic businesses as risky due to new technologies, uncertain markets, or high upfront costs. Impact investors bridge this gap by valuing long-term social and environmental returns alongside financial ones. This approach allows enterprises to experiment, innovate, and refine models until they achieve commercial viability. Blended finance mechanisms, combining public and private funds, further de-risk projects, attracting larger pools of capital to bioeconomic ventures.

The relationship between impact investors and bioeconomic enterprises is not limited to funding. Investors often provide technical expertise, governance support, and access to networks that help businesses expand and build credibility. Partnerships between investors, municipalities, and research institutions create ecosystems where bioeconomic enterprises can thrive. These ecosystems align capital, policy, and innovation, ensuring that enterprises are integrated into broader urban development strategies rather than operating in isolation.

Measuring outcomes is a core element of impact investment in the bioeconomy. Investors seek clear metrics on resource efficiency, emissions reductions, waste diversion, biodiversity impacts, and social inclusion. Bioeconomic enterprises that adopt transparent monitoring and reporting systems are more likely to attract and retain investment. This emphasis on accountability reinforces trust, ensuring that financial flows genuinely advance sustainability rather than superficial "greenwashing."

The growth of impact investment in urban bioeconomy sectors also supports inclusivity and equity. Investments can target enterprises that create jobs in disadvantaged communities, expand access to healthy food, or improve air and water quality in underserved neighborhoods. By prioritizing both financial and social returns, impact investors ensure that bioeconomic growth contributes to reducing inequality rather than exacerbating it.

Impact investment and bioeconomic enterprises together illustrate the potential for aligning finance with regenerative development. By mobilizing capital for businesses that harness biological resources, close resource loops, and deliver social benefits, they help cities transition toward sustainable, circular, and resilient systems. Their partnership ensures that the urban bioeconomy is not only technically feasible but also economically viable and socially just.

Public and Private Sector Financing Mechanisms

Financing mechanisms from both the public and private sectors are essential for advancing the urban bioeconomy, ensuring that innovative projects have the resources needed to move from vision to implementation. Urban bioeconomic initiatives—ranging from biorefineries and green infrastructure to bio-based construction and sustainable transport—often require significant upfront capital and face risks associated with new technologies and markets. Effective financing mechanisms reduce these risks, mobilize investment, and align financial flows with sustainability objectives.

Public sector financing mechanisms often play a catalytic role by creating enabling conditions for bioeconomic projects. Governments can provide grants, subsidies, and concessional loans that lower the financial barriers for early-stage initiatives. Public funds also support research, pilot projects, and demonstration programs that de-risk technologies before they scale commercially. Municipalities can issue green bonds to finance infrastructure such as waste-to-energy plants, urban agriculture systems, and bio-based construction projects. These instruments attract investors by ensuring

89

transparency, accountability, and clear environmental benefits. Public financing also includes tax incentives and rebates, which encourage businesses and consumers to adopt bio-based solutions in areas such as energy efficiency or sustainable materials.

Public-private partnerships further expand financing opportunities by combining government support with private-sector expertise and capital. Governments can share risks by providing guarantees or co-financing, enabling private firms to invest in projects that might otherwise be considered too risky. These partnerships are particularly effective in infrastructure-intensive sectors such as urban energy systems, sustainable transport, and large-scale waste valorization, where coordination and long-term commitments are required. By fostering collaboration, public-private partnerships ensure that projects deliver both public value and private returns.

On the private side, financing mechanisms are increasingly shaped by sustainability considerations. Venture capital, private equity, and impact investors are directing funds toward bioeconomic enterprises that demonstrate both profitability and measurable environmental or social benefits. For startups and small enterprises, these investments provide the seed capital required to bring innovations—such as bio-based plastics, sustainable textiles, or circular food systems—to market. Institutional investors, including pension funds and insurance companies, are also incorporating sustainability criteria into their portfolios, creating demand for bioeconomic projects that meet environmental, social, and governance (ESG) standards.

Commercial banks and financial institutions play a crucial role by offering loans, credit lines, and leasing arrangements tailored to bioeconomic initiatives. Increasingly, banks are developing green finance products that provide favorable terms for projects meeting sustainability benchmarks. Sustainability-linked loans, for instance, reduce borrowing costs for companies that achieve specific environmental performance targets. These instruments align financial incentives with sustainable practices, encouraging businesses to improve efficiency and adopt bio-based innovations.

Blended finance mechanisms, which combine public and private resources, are particularly important for scaling urban bioeconomy projects. Public funds de-risk investments by covering early-stage costs or providing guarantees, while private investors supply the additional capital needed for large-scale implementation. This structure ensures that resources are used efficiently, and that risk is shared in ways that encourage wider participation.

Public and private sector financing mechanisms together create a comprehensive ecosystem for funding the urban bioeconomy. Public funds establish the foundation by reducing risks and signaling policy support, while private capital drives innovation, efficiency, and scaling. By combining these mechanisms through collaboration and innovative instruments, cities can secure the financial resources necessary to transform bioeconomic potential into tangible, sustainable outcomes.

Incentivizing Innovation Through Policy Finance

Policy finance is a critical tool for incentivizing innovation in the urban bioeconomy, shaping the financial and regulatory environment to encourage investment in new technologies, materials, and business models. By combining fiscal measures with targeted funding and supportive regulations, governments can reduce risks, accelerate adoption, and ensure that bio-based solutions are embedded into urban systems. Policy finance aligns public resources with strategic priorities, guiding both public and private capital toward sustainable innovation.

One of the primary ways policy finance incentivizes innovation is through subsidies and grants. These mechanisms lower the costs of research, development, and demonstration, enabling innovators to test new technologies without bearing the full financial burden. For urban bioeconomic initiatives—such as biorefineries, waste-to-energy plants, or vertical farming—grants can cover early-stage expenses that would otherwise deter private investors. Pilot projects supported by public funds also serve as proof of concept, demonstrating feasibility and building investor confidence for larger-scale deployment.

Tax incentives are another powerful instrument. Reduced tax rates, credits, or deductions for bio-based industries encourage companies to invest in sustainable technologies. For example, tax credits for renewable energy generation or deductions for using bio-based materials in construction make these options more competitive against conventional alternatives. At the municipal level, property tax reductions can be offered to developers who integrate green infrastructure or bioeconomic principles into urban projects. These measures create predictable financial advantages that stimulate innovation and adoption.

Policy finance also includes the use of public procurement as a demand-side incentive. Governments can leverage their purchasing power to create stable markets for bio-based products and services. By mandating bio-based packaging in municipal services, requiring renewable construction materials in public buildings, or sourcing food for schools from urban agriculture projects, governments generate demand that encourages private-sector investment and innovation. Procurement policies act as both financial incentives and market signals, steering industries toward sustainable practices.

Loan guarantees and concessional finance provide additional support by reducing risks for private investors. Bioeconomic projects often face uncertainties due to untested markets, technological challenges, or high upfront costs. Public agencies that offer loan guarantees share these risks, making it easier for private firms and banks to finance innovative projects. Concessional loans with lower interest rates or extended repayment periods further ease the financial burden, enabling entrepreneurs to focus on scaling innovations.

Innovation funds and blended finance models strengthen policy finance by pooling resources from public and private actors. Governments can establish dedicated funds for bioeconomic innovation, co-financed by international organizations, impact investors, or development banks. These funds not only provide capital but also signal political commitment, encouraging broader participation. By aligning multiple financing sources, blended models ensure that early-stage risks are shared while long-term rewards are distributed across stakeholders.

Policy finance also plays a role in creating enabling environments for innovation. Support for education, workforce training, and research institutions ensures that cities have the skills and knowledge to drive bioeconomic development. Transparent regulations and clear sustainability standards reduce uncertainty, while monitoring and reporting frameworks ensure accountability. Together, these measures complement financial incentives, creating comprehensive support for innovation ecosystems.

Incentivizing innovation through policy finance ensures that cities can overcome barriers to adopting bio-based solutions. By aligning fiscal tools, procurement strategies, and risk-sharing mechanisms, governments create the conditions for entrepreneurs, businesses, and communities to drive sustainable transformation. These incentives not only accelerate technological progress but also embed circularity and resilience into the fabric of urban development.

Long-Term Economic Benefits of Urban Bioeconomy

The urban bioeconomy offers profound long-term economic benefits by restructuring how cities manage resources, produce goods, and deliver services. Rooted in principles of circularity and renewable resource use, the bioeconomy reduces dependence on finite fossil-based inputs while fostering innovation and resilience. Over time, this systemic shift strengthens urban economies by creating new industries, lowering costs, and improving quality of life for citizens.

One of the most significant economic benefits lies in resource efficiency. Conventional urban systems are highly resource-intensive, generating large amounts of waste and emissions. By transforming waste into inputs—such as biogas from organic residues, compost for agriculture, or bio-based materials from municipal waste—cities reduce costs associated with disposal and imports of raw materials. This circular use of resources not only saves money in the long term but also creates revenue streams from products that were once discarded.

Job creation is another central benefit. The transition to bio-based systems stimulates demand for skilled labor in areas such as biotechnology, sustainable construction, renewable energy, and waste management. New enterprises emerge around urban farming, bio-based packaging, and bio-refineries, generating opportunities across value chains. Unlike jobs tied to fossil-based industries, these roles are resilient to future regulatory, environmental, and market shifts, ensuring sustained employment growth. Training programs and education aligned with the bioeconomy further strengthen the workforce, preparing citizens for long-term participation in innovative industries.

The bioeconomy also reduces economic risks tied to external shocks. Cities dependent on fossil fuels or imported raw materials are vulnerable to supply disruptions, price volatility, and geopolitical tensions. By shifting to locally sourced, renewable biological inputs, urban economies become more self-sufficient and less exposed to these risks. At the same time, resilience to climate change—through green infrastructure, water-sensitive design, and sustainable transport—protects cities from costly damages associated with extreme weather events.

Innovation and competitiveness are further enhanced by the bioeconomy. Investment in research and development accelerates technological breakthroughs, positioning cities as leaders in emerging global markets for bio-based products and services. This leadership attracts private investment, fosters entrepreneurship, and creates spillover benefits across other sectors. Urban centers that adopt bioeconomic strategies early are well placed to influence global standards and capture first-mover advantages in industries such as bio-based materials, sustainable transport, and biotechnology.

Health and well-being improvements also yield long-term economic gains. Bio-based innovations reduce pollution, enhance air and water quality, and support healthier diets, lowering public health costs. Green spaces, bio-based construction materials, and clean energy systems reduce exposure to environmental risks, resulting in savings for healthcare systems and improved productivity. These benefits extend to social cohesion, as more inclusive and sustainable urban environments attract talent and investment.

Over the long term, the urban bioeconomy provides a pathway for cities to align growth with sustainability, creating economies that thrive within ecological limits. By generating efficiency, resilience, jobs, and innovation, the bioeconomy positions urban centers not only to meet immediate challenges but also to secure durable prosperity. Its integration into city systems ensures that economic development goes hand in hand with environmental regeneration and social equity.

Chapter 9: Pathways to Implementation

Pathways to implementation translate the vision of the urban bioeconomy into actionable strategies that cities can adopt to achieve meaningful change. While concepts such as circularity, renewable resource use, and bio-based innovation provide direction, success depends on practical steps that integrate these ideas into urban systems. Implementation requires coordinated planning, phased approaches, and the alignment of stakeholders across government, business, and civil society. This chapter explores the processes, tools, and strategies that guide cities from high-level commitments to tangible outcomes, ensuring that bioeconomic principles become embedded in daily operations and long-term urban development.

Roadmaps for Urban Bioeconomy Transition

Developing roadmaps for the urban bioeconomy transition is essential for guiding cities through the complex process of adopting bio-based and circular systems. Roadmaps serve as structured frameworks that outline goals, milestones, policies, and actions required to embed the bioeconomy into urban development. They help align stakeholders, reduce uncertainty, and ensure that the transition is coherent, measurable, and scalable across multiple sectors.

The first step in designing a roadmap is establishing a clear vision and objectives. Cities must define what the bioeconomy means in their specific context, taking into account local resources, industries, and social needs. For some, the focus may be on valorizing organic waste and producing renewable energy, while others may emphasize bio-based construction or sustainable food systems. Articulating long-term goals such as carbon neutrality, zero waste, or resilient supply chains provides direction and ensures that short-term actions are aligned with broader sustainability outcomes.

Mapping current resource flows is a crucial element of the roadmap. Urban metabolism studies, which analyze how materials, water, and energy move through the city, provide the data needed to identify inefficiencies and opportunities for circularity. By understanding where resources are consumed and wasted, policymakers can prioritize interventions such as nutrient recovery, biorefineries, or green infrastructure. This analytical foundation ensures that decisions are evidence-based and tailored to local conditions.

Roadmaps also need to define pathways and milestones. These intermediate steps break down ambitious long-term visions into achievable stages, allowing for incremental progress while maintaining momentum. For example, a roadmap might begin with pilot projects in waste-to-energy or bio-based packaging, followed by scaling successful initiatives and embedding them into urban planning. Milestones provide benchmarks that help track progress, measure impacts, and adjust strategies as technologies and markets evolve.

Policy and governance frameworks are central to the roadmap process. Clear regulations, incentives, and standards create the enabling environment for innovation and investment. Integrating the bioeconomy into urban master planning ensures that land use, zoning, and infrastructure are aligned with circular principles. At the same time, roadmaps should outline roles and responsibilities for different stakeholders—municipal authorities, businesses, research institutions, and communities—ensuring that all actors are engaged and accountable.

Financing strategies are another critical component. Roadmaps should identify funding mechanisms such as green bonds, impact investment, and public-private partnerships to support both early-stage innovation and large-scale deployment. By linking finance to specific actions and milestones, cities can ensure that resources are available when needed and that investment flows are aligned with bioeconomic priorities.

Public participation and awareness-raising strengthen the legitimacy and effectiveness of roadmaps. Community engagement in shaping goals and monitoring progress fosters ownership and trust. Educational campaigns build understanding of the bioeconomy and encourage behavioral change, ensuring that transitions are supported not only at the institutional level but also within households and neighborhoods.

Roadmaps for the urban bioeconomy transition thus serve as practical guides that connect vision with action. By defining goals, mapping resource flows, setting milestones, aligning policies, mobilizing finance, and engaging citizens, they provide the structure needed to transform cities into regenerative, resilient, and sustainable systems. These roadmaps ensure that the bioeconomy is not just a concept but a concrete pathway to long-term urban transformation.

Stakeholder Engagement and Social Innovation

Stakeholder engagement and social innovation are central to advancing the urban bioeconomy, ensuring that transitions to bio-based and circular systems are inclusive, effective, and aligned with community needs. Because cities are complex systems where governments, businesses, civil society, and citizens interact, building broad coalitions is critical to implementing bioeconomic strategies. Social innovation—new forms of collaboration, governance, and practices that address societal challenges—further strengthens these transitions by fostering creativity and inclusivity. Together, engagement and innovation create the social foundation for sustainable urban transformation.

Stakeholder engagement begins with recognizing the diverse actors involved in urban systems. Municipal governments provide leadership through policies and regulations, but they must coordinate with businesses that develop bio-based products, research institutions that generate knowledge, and civil society organizations that advocate for sustainability. Citizens, as both consumers and producers, play a crucial role in adopting new behaviors such as waste separation, supporting bio-based goods, or participating in urban agriculture. Effective engagement ensures that all these voices are represented, avoiding top-down approaches that may overlook local needs or generate resistance.

Inclusive dialogue is a cornerstone of engagement. Public consultations, participatory planning workshops, and digital platforms allow communities to contribute ideas, express concerns, and shape priorities. This inclusion builds legitimacy and trust, increasing the likelihood that bioeconomic policies and projects will be accepted and supported. Engaging marginalized groups is particularly important, as they often face disproportionate impacts from environmental degradation while being excluded from decision-making processes. By incorporating equity into engagement strategies, cities ensure that the benefits of the bioeconomy are widely shared.

Social innovation complements engagement by fostering new solutions that emerge from collaboration. Community-led initiatives such as cooperative food markets, repair cafés, and local energy cooperatives exemplify how citizens can co-create bioeconomic practices. These innovations reduce dependency on centralized systems while strengthening resilience at the neighborhood level. Digital technologies further expand opportunities for social innovation, enabling peer-to-peer platforms for sharing resources, exchanging knowledge, and supporting local bio-based enterprises.

Partnerships across sectors are another dimension of social innovation. Public-private-community collaborations create ecosystems where experimentation and scaling of bioeconomic projects can flourish. For example, partnerships between municipalities, universities, and local businesses can establish living labs to test bio-based materials, waste-to-energy systems, or green infrastructure in real-world contexts. These collaborative environments generate knowledge, accelerate adoption, and provide models that can be replicated across cities.

Education and capacity building are also crucial. Schools, universities, and vocational programs can integrate bioeconomy concepts into curricula, preparing future generations with the skills needed for emerging industries. Public awareness campaigns that communicate the benefits of bio-based solutions and circular practices help shift consumer behavior. Social innovation thrives when citizens are informed, empowered, and capable of participating actively in transitions.

Governance frameworks must institutionalize stakeholder engagement and support social innovation. Transparent decision-making, accountability mechanisms, and funding for community initiatives create enabling conditions for participation and experimentation. Policies that recognize and support grassroots initiatives ensure that social innovation is not marginalized but integrated into formal urban strategies.

Stakeholder engagement and social innovation therefore form the social infrastructure of the urban bioeconomy. By fostering collaboration, inclusivity, and creativity, they ensure that transitions are not only technically feasible and economically viable but also socially just and widely supported. This foundation is essential for building resilient, circular, and regenerative cities.

Education and Workforce Development

Education and workforce development are critical enablers of the urban bioeconomy, ensuring that cities have the skills, knowledge, and capacity to implement bio-based and circular systems. As the bioeconomy transforms sectors such as energy, waste management, construction, healthcare, and food, it generates demand for new competencies that span biology, engineering, economics, and policy. Preparing current and future workers for these roles requires rethinking education systems, investing in training, and fostering lifelong learning opportunities. Without a skilled and adaptable workforce, the transition to sustainable urban systems cannot be achieved at scale.

Formal education is the foundation of workforce development in the bioeconomy. Schools, universities, and vocational institutions must integrate bioeconomy principles into curricula, exposing students to concepts such as circularity, renewable resources, and biotechnology. Interdisciplinary learning is particularly important, as bioeconomic challenges often require combining knowledge from biology, engineering, and social sciences. For example, students studying urban planning should understand resource efficiency and green infrastructure, while engineering programs should incorporate modules on bio-based materials and waste valorization. Embedding these topics into mainstream education ensures that future professionals are prepared to contribute to the urban bioeconomy.

Vocational and technical training provide practical skills for workers who implement bioeconomic solutions on the ground. Programs in areas such as bioenergy production, wastewater treatment, organic waste valorization, and bio-based construction prepare technicians and operators to manage new technologies. As cities expand their reliance on biorefineries, smart waste systems, and green building practices, demand for skilled labor in these sectors will grow. Ensuring access to vocational training helps create employment opportunities for a wide range of workers, including those transitioning from declining fossil-based industries.

Lifelong learning is another vital dimension of workforce development. The bioeconomy evolves rapidly, driven by technological innovation and shifting policies. Workers must continually update their skills to remain competitive. Cities can foster lifelong learning through online platforms, community training centers, and partnerships with universities and private companies. Providing flexible and accessible opportunities for professional development ensures that the workforce adapts to emerging needs while maintaining inclusivity across age groups and educational backgrounds.

Workforce development is not only about technical skills but also about fostering innovation and entrepreneurship. Education systems should encourage creativity, problem-solving, and collaboration, enabling students and workers to design and scale new bio-based solutions. Incubators, accelerators, and living labs linked to universities or municipalities can provide practical environments for testing innovations and creating new enterprises. By fostering entrepreneurial mindsets, cities cultivate ecosystems where bioeconomic startups and small businesses can thrive.

Governance and policy support are essential to align education and workforce development with bioeconomic goals. Public investment in education programs, scholarships, and research ensures that skills development is prioritized. Partnerships between governments, businesses, and educational institutions help match training with labor market needs. For example, municipalities can collaborate with universities to design specialized programs in bio-based urban systems, while industry can provide apprenticeships and internships that give students hands-on experience.

Education and workforce development therefore act as the backbone of the urban bioeconomy. By preparing workers with the knowledge and skills needed for circular and bio-based systems, cities not only enable the transition but also create inclusive opportunities for economic growth. A well-trained and adaptable workforce ensures that the benefits of the bioeconomy extend across society, building the human capacity required for resilient, sustainable urban futures.

Measuring Progress and Monitoring Systems

Measuring progress and implementing effective monitoring systems are essential for ensuring that the transition to the urban bioeconomy delivers tangible and lasting results. Cities face complex challenges in aligning economic growth with environmental sustainability, and without reliable tools to track outcomes, policies risk falling short of their objectives. Monitoring systems provide the data needed to evaluate effectiveness, improve accountability, and adjust strategies in response to emerging challenges and opportunities.

A key element of measuring progress is defining clear indicators that reflect bioeconomic principles. Indicators should cover environmental, social, and economic dimensions to capture the full scope of transformation. Environmental indicators might include reductions in greenhouse gas emissions, increases in renewable energy use, diversion of organic waste from landfills, or improvements in water reuse rates. Social indicators could track job creation in bio-based sectors, access to sustainable food systems, or public participation in circular initiatives. Economic indicators assess growth in bio-based industries, investment flows, and cost savings from resource efficiency. Together, these metrics ensure that monitoring reflects both ecological sustainability and social well-being.

Data collection is central to monitoring systems. Cities can draw on multiple sources, including municipal records, satellite imagery, smart sensors, and citizen reporting. Smart technologies such as Internet of Things devices provide real-time data on energy consumption, waste flows, and water usage, enabling rapid analysis and response. Open data platforms allow stakeholders to access and interpret information, fostering transparency and collaboration. Integrating these tools creates a robust data ecosystem that supports informed decision-making and continuous learning.

Monitoring systems also benefit from adopting adaptive frameworks. The urban bioeconomy is dynamic, shaped by technological innovation, changing behaviors, and external shocks such as climate events or economic crises. Static metrics may fail to capture these shifts. Adaptive monitoring uses regular reviews, scenario planning, and feedback loops to ensure that indicators remain relevant and that policies can be adjusted quickly. This flexibility makes monitoring a tool not only for evaluation but also for resilience and innovation.

Governance plays a decisive role in institutionalizing monitoring systems. Municipal authorities must establish clear responsibilities for data collection, analysis, and reporting. Independent oversight bodies or partnerships with universities and research institutions can enhance credibility and technical capacity. At the same time, stakeholder participation is crucial. Involving communities, businesses, and civil society in defining indicators and interpreting results ensures that monitoring reflects diverse priorities and builds trust in the process.

International frameworks provide additional guidance for measuring progress. Aligning urban bioeconomy monitoring with global standards such as the United Nations Sustainable Development Goals or the European Union's circular economy indicators allows cities to benchmark performance and share best practices. This alignment also makes it easier to attract funding, as investors and development agencies seek measurable outcomes tied to recognized frameworks.

Measuring progress and monitoring systems thus serve as the backbone of accountability and effectiveness in the urban bioeconomy. By establishing clear indicators, leveraging technology, enabling adaptive management, and fostering transparency, cities ensure that their bioeconomic transitions are both measurable and meaningful. These systems provide the evidence needed to demonstrate impact, refine strategies, and sustain momentum toward regenerative and resilient urban futures.

Global Lessons for Local Action

The urban bioeconomy is not a one-size-fits-all model; its success depends on tailoring global experiences to the specific contexts of individual cities. Around the world, cities are experimenting with circular resource management, bio-based materials, sustainable transport, and innovative governance frameworks. These global experiences offer valuable lessons that can inspire and inform local action, enabling cities to avoid pitfalls, adopt proven practices, and accelerate their own transitions. Learning from others while adapting solutions to local conditions is key to building resilient and regenerative urban systems.

One global lesson is the importance of integrating waste management into circular value chains. Cities in Europe and Asia have demonstrated how policies mandating waste separation and recycling can support the development of bio-based industries, such as composting, anaerobic digestion, and bioplastics. Local governments can adapt these strategies by implementing source-separation systems, investing in organic waste valorization, and creating markets for bio-based products. The principle is clear: treating waste as a resource builds the foundation for the bioeconomy, but implementation must consider local infrastructure, cultural practices, and financial capacities.

Another lesson comes from the role of innovation and technology in urban bioeconomy transitions. Smart cities across North America and Asia are using digital tools to monitor energy, water, and waste flows in real time, improving efficiency and reducing resource consumption. These experiences show how technology can amplify bioeconomic strategies, but they also highlight the need for strong governance, data protection, and community trust. Local action should not simply copy technological solutions but should focus on how they can be integrated into existing systems and aligned with citizen priorities.

Global experiences also underscore the importance of policy frameworks and long-term planning. Countries in the European Union have adopted circular economy roadmaps that set measurable targets for waste reduction, renewable energy, and bio-based industries. These provide clear signals for investment and innovation. Cities elsewhere can learn from this structured approach by developing localized bioeconomy roadmaps with context-specific goals, milestones, and monitoring systems. The lesson is that ambitious yet flexible planning is critical to sustaining momentum and ensuring accountability.

Equity and inclusivity represent another important lesson. In Latin America and Africa, community-driven initiatives such as urban farming cooperatives and informal recycling networks demonstrate how grassroots innovation contributes to bioeconomic transitions.

These examples highlight the importance of involving marginalized groups and recognizing their contributions. Local action can replicate this inclusive approach by ensuring that policies and financing mechanisms support community enterprises, generate local jobs, and distribute benefits equitably across urban populations.

Finally, international collaboration offers lessons in scaling and integration. Networks of cities engaged in sustainability, such as C40 or ICLEI, provide platforms for knowledge exchange, joint projects, and shared advocacy. Participation in such networks helps local governments access global expertise and financing, while also contributing their own insights to global debates. The lesson for local actors is that engaging in global dialogues strengthens local transitions by connecting them to broader movements and resources.

Global lessons for local action demonstrate that the urban bioeconomy is both a shared and a context-specific endeavor. By adapting global best practices in waste valorization, technology, policy planning, inclusivity, and collaboration, cities can design pathways that reflect their unique challenges and opportunities. This exchange of knowledge ensures that the urban bioeconomy evolves as a collective project, where local actions are informed by global experience and global progress is enriched by local innovation.

Conclusion

The urban bioeconomy represents a transformative framework for rethinking how cities use resources, design systems, and plan for the future. By embedding principles of circularity, renewable resource use, and regenerative design, it offers a pathway to address the pressing challenges of urbanization, climate change, and social inequality. More than a technical shift, it is a systemic reorientation of how cities function, linking waste to value creation, aligning growth with ecological limits, and fostering innovation across multiple sectors.

The long-term benefits of adopting bioeconomic approaches in cities are far-reaching. By reusing water, recovering nutrients, and valorizing organic waste, urban systems reduce dependence on finite resources while cutting emissions and pollution. Bio-based materials and energy solutions not only replace fossil-based alternatives but also create new industries and jobs, strengthening resilience against economic and environmental shocks. Education, workforce development, and stakeholder engagement ensure that these transitions are inclusive, equipping communities with the skills and opportunities to thrive in emerging bio-based economies.

Governance, financing, and international collaboration provide the enabling structures to make the urban bioeconomy a reality. Policy frameworks that incentivize innovation, sustainable finance instruments that mobilize capital, and research and development ecosystems that drive technological breakthroughs all contribute to building momentum. At the same time, lessons from global experiences guide local action, ensuring that strategies are tailored to context while benefiting from shared knowledge. Monitoring systems and adaptive planning guarantee that progress is measurable, accountable, and responsive to change.

The urban bioeconomy is not a distant vision but a practical pathway already unfolding in cities worldwide. By integrating biotechnology, green infrastructure, sustainable food systems, and renewable energy into everyday urban life, it shows how ecological and economic priorities can reinforce one another. The transition requires commitment, creativity, and collaboration across all levels of society, but the rewards are resilient, low-carbon, and inclusive cities that serve both people and the planet.

As cities continue to grow, the urban bioeconomy provides a blueprint for aligning human development with nature's regenerative cycles. It is both an economic strategy and a societal commitment to building futures that are sustainable, equitable, and thriving within ecological boundaries.

www.ingramcontent.com/pod-product-compliance
Lightning Source LLC
Chambersburg PA
CBHW052139270326
41930CB00012B/2951